# *LET US NOW SPEAK OF EXTINCTION*

A QUASI-PHILOSOPHICAL RANT IN
MICROS ON DEATH AND ASSORTED
OTHER AMUSING THINGS

## Michael C. Keith

MADHAT PRESS
ASHEVILLE, NORTH CAROLINA

MadHat Press
MadHat Incorporated
PO Box 8364, Asheville, NC 28814

Copyright © 2018 Michael C. Keith
All rights reserved

The Library of Congress has assigned this edition a Control Number of 2018944949

ISBN 978-1-941196-70-0 (paperback)

Text by Michael C. Keith
Author photograph by Dana Marshall
Cover design by Marc Vincenz
Cover image: *Bicycle Acrobats* (1917) by Charles Demuth (1883–1935)

www.madhat-press.com

First Printing

# LET US NOW SPEAK OF EXTINCTION

# Other works of fiction by Michael C. Keith

*Perspective Drifts Like a Log on a River*

*Slow Transit*

*Bits, Specks, Crumbs, Flecks*

*The Near Enough*

*If Things Were Made to Last Forever*

*Caricatures*

*The Collector of Tears*

*Everything is Epic*

*Sad Boy*

*Of Night and Light*

*Hoag's Object*

*And Through the Trembling Air*

*Life is Falling Sideways*

Michael C. Keith is also the author of an acclaimed memoir (*The Next Better Place*, Algonquin Books) and two dozen non-fiction titles focusing on topics in mass communication.

*With special thanks to George Ovitt, who saw this collection before anyone and did something about it.*

# Table of Contents

| | |
|---|---|
| The Silver Lining | 1 |
| In Praise of Xanax | 2 |
| Discount Giants | 3 |
| Forced Learning | 4 |
| Falling Stars | 5 |
| The Evolution of Symbiotic Relationships in English Composition | 6 |
| Troubled Sleep | 7 |
| Oblivious | 8 |
| Not Up for Debate | 9 |
| His Precious Ordinary | 10 |
| The Absence of Job Satisfaction | 11 |
| Condolence Pastry | 12 |
| It's the Way His Life Went with His Smartphone | 13 |
| Consultation | 14 |
| A Damn Awful Thing to Realize at 70 | 15 |
| And This Is the Way Bad Shit Starts | 16 |
| A Time and Place for Everything | 17 |
| Wind Instrument | 18 |
| Early Signs of a Criminal Life | 19 |
| WYO 287 | 20 |
| Sad Baby | 21 |
| Jack Kerouac's Girlfriend Wrote This: | 22 |
| Classroom Success | 23 |
| *His* Paris | 24 |
| Don't Let Strangers with Crazy Eyes into Your Crazy House | 25 |
| Empathy | 26 |
| First Trip to Orlando | 27 |
| You Never Know Everything about Your Friends | 28 |
| Them Texans Love to Grill | 29 |

| | |
|---|---|
| Seeking Information | 30 |
| Darkest Before Dawn | 31 |
| An Imagined Conversation Between Heinrich Himmler and Hugo Boss on the Occasion of the Initial Meeting Concerning the Design of the SS Headwear Medallion | 32 |
| She Came Back | 33 |
| Surrounded by Family and Friends | 34 |
| Diplomacy | 35 |
| Clay Was Someone Who Always Went for It | 36 |
| What's in a Name? | 37 |
| Downsizing | 38 |
| Adjusting One's Priorities | 39 |
| It Is Said We Have More in Common than We Do Our Differences | 40 |
| Sometimes It Takes … | 41 |
| You Bet Your Life | 42 |
| Go Fuck Yourself, Cuz! | 43 |
| When Reprisal Backfires and You Look the Fool Again | 44 |
| Irresponsible Parenting | 45 |
| When an Appropriate Level of Sympathy Goes Missing | 46 |
| So Close but Yet … | 47 |
| Self-Immolation | 48 |
| Postmortem Fetal Extrusion | 49 |
| Sometimes a Little Compromise Is All It Takes | 50 |
| Obit | 51 |
| When Things Don't Add Up | 52 |
| Fuck Them! | 53 |
| End Date | 54 |
| Foe | 55 |
| Scent | 56 |
| From That Moment On | 58 |
| Old Clip on YouTube | 59 |

| | |
|---|---|
| Temporary Measures | 60 |
| On Possessing a Belief in the Secret Powers of Friends | 61 |
| A Process of Elimination | 62 |
| Degrading: Attack au Fer | 63 |
| On Deferring a Decision in the Face of Likely Annihilation | 64 |
| One Must Expect Change | 65 |
| Small but Meaningful Consolation | 66 |
| Farewell Soirée | 67 |
| When It Appears You've Been Blessed with Good Fortune but You're Mistaken | 68 |
| *You Can't Go Home Again* | 69 |
| When the Dead Speak, They May Say Something You Don't Want to Hear | 70 |
| When Pets Surprise You | 72 |
| NASA Retrieves a Message from an Extraterrestrial Object | 73 |
| Awareness | 74 |
| In the Order of Importance | 75 |
| What You Don't Have ... | 76 |
| Putting Up with the Inconveniences of a Paradise | 77 |
| Silver Lining | 78 |
| Frontier Justice | 79 |
| An Unsettling Comment | 80 |
| Sometimes Something Opens a Door Long Closed | 81 |
| Message to Earth by Sustenance Harvesters from Another World | 82 |
| Coping Behavior | 83 |
| Two-O'Clock Jump | 84 |
| Doubt Is the Enemy of Creativity* | 85 |
| Dreams Can Be Just That | 86 |
| Pre-emptive Strike | 87 |
| Encounter with a Stranger in a Big City | 88 |
| Gratitude | 89 |

| | |
|---|---|
| Hermantage | 90 |
| Disregarding Bad News | 91 |
| Everyone Has a Price | 92 |
| Lost in Space | 94 |
| Variation | 95 |
| "One Good Deed Is Not Enough to Redeem a Man from a Lifetime of Wickedness" | 96 |
| "Where you going?" asked the driver to the hitchhiker. | 97 |
| Henry Had Ambitions Thwarted by the Effects of Time | 98 |
| Why Frank Failed as a Creator of Word Puzzles | 99 |
| Authorities in New Dawn, Vermont, Break with Procedure | 100 |
| Insomnia | 101 |
| Price Over Prejudice | 102 |
| Wake Up, for Christ's Sake! | 103 |
| He Died While She Was Gone | 104 |
| Bad Chemistry | 105 |
| Motives Can Be Difficult to Fathom | 106 |
| Animus | 107 |
| Is More Information Necessary? | 108 |
| Feel the Beat | 109 |
| Cotillion of the Fittest | 110 |
| When the Right Thing to Do Doesn't Seem Quite Right | 111 |
| Global Scourge | 113 |
| How Atheism Flourished in Modern Times | 114 |
| A Happy Realization | 115 |
| One Good Deed … | 116 |
| What the Minister Said That Disturbed His Congregation | 117 |
| Coming to Terms | 118 |
| Canine I.Q. | 119 |
| Sequel | 120 |

| | |
|---|---|
| Time Is a Joy-Killer | 121 |
| Party Pooper | 122 |
| Mrs. Johnson Is Ready to Greet the Future | 123 |
| Vacationland | 124 |
| Fourth and Powell | 125 |
| Second Thoughts | 126 |
| Compassion Lessons | 127 |
| When Reason Goes Out the Car Window | 128 |
| Sneaky Pete | 129 |
| It's All in the Numbers | 130 |
| The Rapprochement | 131 |
| Less Than Expected | 132 |
| A Statement That Failed to Comfort a Reluctant Flyer | 133 |
| It's Only a Matter of Time Before Your Body Turns Lethal | 134 |
| Words Pertaining to the Final Human Indignation | 135 |
| Let Us Now Speak of Extinction | 136 |
| One with Nature | 137 |
| Seeking Counsel | 138 |
| Locating Dreams | 139 |
| Hurt | 140 |
| The Question That Stumped the Lesser Einstein | 141 |
| New Movement | 142 |
| If Wishes Were Buses, Little Girls Would Ride | 143 |
| Timeless Injustice | 144 |
| Cliques | 145 |
| My Final Curtain … | 146 |
| The Joy of Parenthood | 147 |
| When Asked by Police Why He Did It, He Replied: | 148 |
| There Are Times When It Is Difficult to Know What to Believe | 149 |
| Never Stand in the Path of the Wheat Thresher | 150 |
| What If the Iceman Didn't Cometh? | 151 |

| | |
|---|---:|
| One Man's Hell | 152 |
| It Should Happen to Me | 153 |
| Objectively | 154 |
| Everlasting Benefit | 155 |
| One Can Learn a Great Deal In-Flight | 156 |
| Salesman of the Year | 157 |
| Alien Invasion | 159 |
| There Are Some Customers Who Simply Cannot Be Pleased | 160 |
| Not Exactly the Same Thing | 161 |
| Sacred Ground | 162 |
| One of Life's Mysteries | 163 |
| Absurd | 164 |
| Happy Hour | 165 |
| Who's Crying Now? | 166 |
| Noah Manages a Final Journal Entry | 167 |
| What the Rabbi Told Him Momentarily Stilled His Fears | 168 |
| Tea Time | 169 |
| Age Non Sequitur | 170 |
| The Enchanting Hereafter | 171 |
| Pointers from Papa | 172 |
| Passing It Along | 173 |
| Profound Discourse at a Dunkin | 174 |
| Something Left to Brag About | 175 |
| On a Late Sunday Afternoon | 176 |
| Paradise Lost | 177 |
| Strategy for Living | 178 |
| Down the Toilet | 179 |
| Afterlife | 180 |
| Hospital Roommates with Contrasting Perspectives | 181 |
| Scything You Up | 182 |
| Six-Foot Variance | 183 |
| There Are Times When You Have to Try a Little Harder | 184 |
| Misconception | 185 |

| | |
|---|---|
| Sensible Eating and Long Life | 186 |
| Vlad's Repast | 187 |
| We All Have Something in Common | 188 |
| The Socially Conscious Sixties | 189 |
| Method of Reconciliation | 190 |
| Nietzsche said, "Without music, life would be a mistake." | 191 |
| Houdini Has a Jarring Wake-Up Call | 192 |
| Late Afternoon of the Writer's Day | 193 |
| Friends with Solutions | 194 |
| Interspection | 195 |
| A Tasteless Offense | 196 |
| Just Look at Us | 197 |
| 3 AM | 198 |
| Accessory | 199 |
| Nature *Boy* | 200 |
| Thoughts That Keep Them Awake | 201 |
| Things Always Make More Sense in the Morning | 202 |
| Someone Has an Emergency and Triggers a Paranoid Reaction | 203 |
| She Asked This Question on Our First Date | 204 |
| It's Good When God Favors You | 205 |
| Old Friends on the Road, Again | 206 |
| The Harsh Realist | 207 |
| Parental Care | 208 |
| The Joy *That* Publishing Brings | 209 |
| Belated Mourning | 210 |
| Stretching the Limits of Acceptance | 211 |
| An Imagined Conversation Between Janis, Jim and Jimi in 2020 | 212 |
| *Everything Old Is New, Again* | 214 |
| In Response to Tragic News of a Global Nature | 215 |
| You Must Plan Ahead When You're Not Quite Like Indigenous Life Forms | 216 |
| Sacrificing for Art | 217 |

| | |
|---|---|
| Imposition | 218 |
| Highway to Heaven | 219 |
| Bedeviled | 220 |
| The Benefits of a Creative Imagination | 221 |
| Animal on the Run | 222 |
| Eternal Question | 223 |
| Maybe God? | 224 |
| Upon Discovering that Author Larry Brown Died in 2004, I Think ... | 225 |
| Pride for Things Not Yours | 226 |
| What Was Outside Comes In | 227 |
| Senior Conundrum | 228 |
| Afterwords | 229 |
| *About the Author* | 231 |

*Waking at four to soundless dark, I stare.*
*In time the curtain-edges will grow light.*
*Till then I see what's really always there:*
*Unresting death, a whole day nearer now.*

—Philip Larkin

*Since we're all going to die, it's obvious that when and where don't matter.*

—Albert Camus

*99.9% of all species ever to have existed on earth have gone extinct.*
*Some design, huh(?)*

—Christopher Hitchens

# The Silver Lining

It seemed to Sol everything that made his life worthwhile was coming to an end. His retirement after 45 years as the comptroller of the Montclair Fabric Company was at hand, and his lifelong passion for numismatics had faded over the past couple of years. But what had contributed most to the quality of his existence was his wife, and now she was in the final stage of a terminal illness. "What will I do?" lamented Sol, and then he reminded himself of the $25 gift certificate to Ruby Tuesday's he'd tucked away in his wallet.

*Michael C. Keith*

# In Praise of Xanax

My heart was about to explode, and I thought about jumping from my speeding car. Then I dug a pill out of my shirt pocket and swallowed it. When I got to the next intersection, I threw the driver in the car next to me the peace sign. I can't say enough about the new class of fast-acting benzodiazepines.

# Discount Giants

Is there a place where you can give back fear, trade it in for something less distressing? It's doing me no good, as far as I can tell, so I should be able to return it. I don't recall where or how I got it, but I've had it for a long time. It's still like new, though, so surely someone will take it back. I've tried Wal-Mart and Target, but they claim it's not one of their items. Maybe Costco?

# Forced Learning

"Gambling wasn't always what drew people to Reno, Nevada," says Clark, adding, "Initially it was a mining, farming, and railroad community."

He mentions stuff like that all of the time. Like for instance, yesterday he stated that Greta Garbo's real name was Lovisa Gustafsson. I don't even know who Greta Garbo is and really don't care.

Another time, Clark explained that what makes Denver the Mile-High City is the 13th step on the west side of the State Capitol Building. Again, it was information I didn't need.

I figure it's important for him to share what he knows with me, so I don't say anything. Besides, you need to get along with your cellmate, especially if he's a pathological didactic.

## Falling Stars

Margaret stared up at the sky and tried to find the constellations she'd learned as a child, like Orion, Ursa Minor, and Cassiopeia. It was a clear night, but she could not locate them. *Well, things do change,* she reasoned.

*Michael C. Keith*

# The Evolution of Symbiotic Relationships in English Composition

### One Character in a Sentence

Margaret said she felt so alone and isolated.

\* \* \*

### Two Characters in a Sentence

Brad and Carl were glad they bumped into each other.

\* \* \*

### Three Characters in a Sentence

Jason and Carmen told Sam that three is a crowd.

# Troubled Sleep

In the morning, she says the intruder reminded her of the Grim Reaper. "He had this big sword in his hand and he was holding it up like he was getting ready to chop us," she recalls." Her dreams are vivid, and some like this one are just plain terrifying. It had my heart pounding because I thought she wasn't dreaming and that someone actually was standing in the doorway of our bedroom about to kill us. After awhile my eyes adjusted enough to the darkness to see there was no one there. "You're having a nightmare," I told her, but she said she wasn't. I got up to pee, and when I came back to bed, she was mumbling something about a giant spider on the wall.

*Michael C. Keith*

## Oblivious

There were body parts all over the place. Like arms and legs, even a head. And blood on the sidewalks and bus bench. There were loud, agonized cries, too. I just kept on driving to the mall so I wouldn't miss meeting up with my girlfriend for supper. When I got there, she asked if I'd heard about the terrorist attack. *Oh, that's what it was,* I thought.

## Not Up for Debate

My friend says, "According to doctors, if you're taking Prilosec every day for heartburn, you may end up with Alzheimer's."

I reply, "Yeah, and plumbers say if you use Drano too much to unclog your drains you could get leaky pipes."

We both think on what the other has said and then continue sealcoating the driveway in silence.

## His Precious Ordinary

Kent wrote the last words to his novel *Plains Folk* and pushed the computer keyboard away in a gesture of finality. He then swung around in his chair and looked at the shelf of books he'd authored over the course of his career. There were a half dozen of them, not counting the foreign editions and paperback versions of the hardcovers. "Got you guys another companion," he said." After a few moments, he stood and stretched his aging body, tapping his forefinger against the porcelain shade of the ceiling light fixture. "Hope this one is good company, because it may be the last," he added, leaving his office and flipping the light switch on his way out.

# The Absence of Job Satisfaction

Jarod ran the elevator in the two-floor, four-room Ames Hotel. His shift was midnight to seven. During that time, the management required that all the outside doors in the building be locked and guests remain in their rooms. Jarod frequently complained of feeling useless.

*Michael C. Keith*

## Condolence Pastry

Sheila found a cinnamon-apple crisp in the back of her refrigerator. At first, she couldn't figure out how it got there. Then she remembered her neighbor had left it on her doorstep after her husband's fatal heart attack nearly two weeks ago. She wondered if it was still good and, after sniffing it, concluded it was. Her appetite had been nonexistent since the funeral and she suddenly felt its return. She began nibbling at the crust of the rediscovered confection and soon was gobbling it with unrestrained enthusiasm. Finally, it dawned on her that she could eat all of the sweets she wanted now that her killjoy husband was no longer around to stop her.

# It's the Way His Life Went with His Smartphone

There it is. Yup, there it is. "Updated two minutes ago." *Click.* "Updated just now."

## Consultation

I told my gerontologist, "I feel like hell in the morning. Aches and pains in every part of my body."

He said, "Well, that's you rotting."

"Terrible way to put it, doc," I replied.

He answered, "Yes, okay, how about this? Your body is undergoing a process called senescence. That's the gradual deterioration of every organ and limb in your anatomy."

*Better,* I thought.

# A Damn Awful Thing to Realize at 70

He thought: *I don't have an authentic personality. It's all smoke and mirrors, surface and artiface ... masquerade.*

*Michael C. Keith*

# AND THIS IS THE WAY BAD SHIT STARTS

Cy noticed a Marlboro on his wife Karen's dresser—it had been the preferred brand of her longtime habit. She'd quit smoking a decade earlier, so naturally it aroused his curiosity, if not suspicion. When he asked her about it, she reacted with a guilty chuckle, claiming she'd had it in her jewelry box for years.

"I kept it in case I had a sudden nicotine attack. Kind of like an alcoholic keeps a bottle of liquor around ... a security-blanket thing. It just made me feel better knowing it was there. Like you haven't been completely abandoned by something you depended on, and if you suddenly go crazy for it, it's there."

Cy smelled the cigarette and tossed it back on the dresser.

"It's fresh. No way you've had it for years. What's going on? You're smoking again, aren't you?"

"I'm not. I had it wrapped tightly so it wouldn't dry up. I'm not lying. It's no big deal," protested Karen, throwing the cigarette in the trash.

"I don't believe you. You were doing it behind my back. What else have you been doing behind my back?"

# A Time and Place for Everything

Meg and Barney Wilde entered the Ace Diner between lunch and suppertime and were told by the manager that he did not condone eating between meals.

*Michael C. Keith*

## WIND INSTRUMENT

The ridge that loomed over the Iverson's cabin on their 25,000-acre sheep ranch in northern Wyoming was called Symphony Rock. Depending on the velocity of the gusts, various melodies—all rooted in music of the classical tradition—emanated from it. This occasioned the departure of all three Iverson children when each turned 18 because of their desire for a more contemporary playlist.

# Early Signs of a Criminal Life

When the prison therapist asked Wayne what was something from his childhood that really angered him, he was told by the young convict that it was when the movie-house manager pointed at him to come up on the stage to help draw the winning number for a year's free pass to the Saturday afternoon matinees and when he started up to the stage, he was told "No ... not *you!* The boy *next* to you." He was so embarrassed and disappointed he wanted to do something terrible to the man, and when he got home he punched his little brother and poured applesauce over his baby sister's head.

*Michael C. Keith*

## WYO 287

I'm taking a motorcycle ride north from Laramie. It's still chilly even though it's early June. The winds are really whipping across Como Bluff as I near the "world's oldest building"—according to *Ripley's Believe It or Not*. It's made of dinosaur bones, so I guess there's some truth to the claim. It used to be a tourist stop that sold artifacts, namely fossils unearthed in the area. I'm disappointed to discover it's closed, since the main reason I've made the trip up is to buy another chunk of dinosaur carcass needed to complete a set of bookends. There's an adjacent structure on the buffeted property, and it's deserted as well. For a time, I peruse the site wondering why such a unique place would be abandoned. *Sad*, I think, returning to the building that was the store. When I peer into one of its dust-covered windows, I can just make out the pelvis of a Stegosaurus.

## Sad Baby

Mildred Jennifer Carlyle was born at Cedars of Lebanon Hospital at 8:37 PM, Monday, November 14, 1949. She was five pounds, seven ounces, and had thick dark hair. She cried the moment she left her mother's womb and continued crying throughout her childhood and adult years. She did, however, stop crying when she was struck by lightning. People wondered if even God had had enough of her incessant blubbering.

*Michael C. Keith*

## JACK KEROUAC'S GIRLFRIEND WROTE THIS:

"The dark had come down over the river like thick black velvet. Here and there at the ends of dead-end streets were dim taverns all brown inside, with dockworkers and sailors steadily drinking under yellow lights. There were no women in this nighttime world."*

I think, *why is he more famous than she is?*

*Joyce Johnson, *Minor Characters,* New York: Penguin Books, 1999, p. 138. (National Book Critics Circle Award winner)

## Classroom Success

The philosophy professor asked the student to provide an example of an axiomatic statement. The student responded, "To be human is to shit your pants." The professor, beaming with approval, declared, "That, young man, earns you an A for the course."

## *His* Paris

He wants to be from there, but he's not. If he moves there, will he be from there, he wonders?

# Don't Let Strangers with Crazy Eyes into Your Crazy House

So he swiveled me around in my chair and slashed me again. Four times he cut me, and I was beginning to lose a lot of blood.

"You want me to stop, just tell me what I want to know," he said, holding back from cutting me a fifth time.

"Okay ... *okay,* I'll tell you what you want," I moaned, hurting too much to hold out any longer.

He backed up a couple steps and lowered the blade.

"So, mister? I'm waiting."

"All right, how about this? *When the sun rises, everything will be brighter,*" I said.

"You sure about that? Absolutely certain?" he hissed, leaning into me.

His breath smelled like something dead.

"Yes, totally," I answered.

The last thing I remember before passing out was the smile on his face.

*Michael C. Keith*

# Empathy

The Seltzers got a call from a friend near noon telling them that their next-door neighbor's nine-year-old daughter had died from anaphylactic shock. Apparently, a bee had gotten into her room late at night and stung her while she slept. Her parents didn't hear her cry … if, in fact, she had cried. Mrs. Seltzer immediately went to her own daughter's room to see if she was ready to go to the mall.

## First Trip to Orlando

It was just before sunset in the Magic Kingdom, and the hotel lobby was empty, except for Tinker Bell and me. I watched as she fluttered around the concierge's desk. She really was a sight to behold—adorable. I was intrigued, if not mesmerized, by her aerobatics and pixie-dust contrail. Then she took notice of me and began to buzz around my head. At first, I didn't mind, but then it got to be annoying. I asked her to stop, but she ignored my request. Finally, I'd had enough and tore her little wings off. It didn't make me feel good to do that, but I was at a loss as to what to do otherwise. My friends think what I did was awful, and now they call me Mr. Faerie Killer. I suppose I'll hear from Disney. They should train their characters to respect the space of strangers.

*Michael C. Keith*

## You Never Know Everything about Your Friends

"Hey, Malcolm, you know how you make a fist, right ... clenching your fingers together like this?" asked Barry, forming a ball with his hand.

"Of course, anyone can do that."

"Well, not like Craig. He curls his fingers in the opposite direction. I mean, they go backwards onto the other side of his hands and look like hoops."

"Huh?"

"No, really. When he noticed I saw him do that, he looked at me weird ... worried. Like he didn't want me to tell anybody he could do that."

"You wouldn't ... *would* you?" asked Malcolm.

"What?"

"Say anything about *this?*"

When his friend rotated his head two full circles without moving the rest of his body, Barry decided to get the hell out of there.

## Them Texans Love to Grill

The old rancher followed his quarry deep into the canyon as the sun fell behind its jagged peaks. The blisters inside his boots and the snake bite to his calf forced him to rest once again before continuing his pursuit of whoever had stolen his new Weber Genesis LX E-340 Liquid Propane Barbecue from his patio. He'd lost his horse to a leg injury after it had stumbled trying to avoid the rattler along the trail. It was a major setback to him, but now he was determined more than ever to catch the culprit who had taken from him what was most precious in his life.

## Seeking Information

He often wondered what the moments after death were like. Was there something wonderful on the other side, or was it simply an immeasurable void? He couldn't find anyone with first-hand knowledge to provide him with an answer.

# Darkest Before Dawn

Ninety-three-year-old Millicent Dubois was deteriorating rapidly. Her left hand was numb, as was her left leg from the knee down. The vision in her right eye was significantly poorer than her left, and her lower back ached more than it had the day before. By midday, she had a terrible headache and a nosebleed that spoiled the front of her dressing gown. Her appetite was nearly nonexistent at suppertime, and the cup of broth she sipped gave her severe heartburn. At bedtime, her vertigo had returned with a vengeance, and she was unable to lie down without becoming quite nauseated. Just before falling to sleep in her hospital room's recliner, her breathing became labored and she was given oxygen. When she woke up 20 minutes later, she told the attending nurse she'd had a great night's sleep and asked if she could go out and play with the rest of the children.

Michael C. Keith

# An Imagined Conversation Between Heinrich Himmler and Hugo Boss on the Occasion of the Initial Meeting Concerning the Design of the SS Headwear Medallion

"So, *Reichsführer*, what is your vision for the insignia that will adorn your officer's visor cap?" asked Hugo Boss, the Nazi Party's foremost fashion designer.

"Well, of course, I want something that symbolizes what we're all about," answered Himmler.

"Yes ... yes, you've made it most clear what you're all about. So, how about a skull and crossbones?"

"Hmm, I'm not sure. It may be a bit too jaunty."

## She Came Back

Viewers tuning into the news learned that a coroner in San Bernardino had irrefutable evidence that a person he'd declared dead 24 hours earlier was alive. How the women, who'd suffered partial decapitation in a car accident, had been restored to life was beyond the explanation of the medical examiner. She'd been found sitting up, head dangling against her chest, in a refrigerated body drawer of the city's morgue when staff returned from lunch. When asked if she recalled anything during the time she was officially dead, she responded, "Yerse."

*Michael C. Keith*

# Surrounded by Family and Friends

The last thing Frank Gilliam wanted was to pass away in full view of everybody. The very idea disgusted him. Indeed, it struck him as a horrible embarrassment to be center-stage when perishing. He agreed that while it was often a dramatic—if not melodramatic—event, it was also completely debasing to have all eyes on you at a time when you likely looked worse than you ever had. *Does anybody look good after withering away in old age or at the end of a long illness,* he reasoned? Thus, he gave strict instructions to be left alone in his last moments of life. So when it appeared he was on the very threshold of oblivion, his health-care agent advised everyone to leave his bedside. After a half hour, the group of mourners was allowed to return to pay their last respects to the dearly departed. When they entered the room, they were shocked at what they found. Gilliam was sitting up in his bed still very much alive. "That was a rehearsal," he said in a barely discernible voice.

## Diplomacy

The long-time, heated debate in Zagreb about who made the best *Strukli* ended when an American tourist sampling several examples of the dish at a local festival said they all tasted like *povracati* to him.

*Michael C. Keith*

# CLAY WAS SOMEONE WHO ALWAYS WENT FOR IT

Friends and relatives thought his extreme curiosity and devil-may-care attitude were dangerous things, since they had put him into some bad situations—a couple had nearly cost him his life. Now, as he sat in his car on a deserted stretch of Montana lowland blacktop, he contemplated doing something he was aware could have dire consequences. He'd weighed the pros and cons and decided to go for it, because he believed the potential rewards extraordinary ... in fact, beyond imagining—immortality, incalculable wealth, sensual fulfillment, and so on. He saw it as a once-in-a-lifetime opportunity, and he felt if he passed it up, he'd regret it forever. *Pooh on those who think I'm foolhardy and impetuous. I did what I felt was right in the past and wouldn't do anything differently now if I had a chance. I survived,* he told himself. With that, he took a deep breath, climbed from his car, weaved his way around the bodies of the scorched prairie dogs, waded through the ankle-deep noxious effluvium, and moved up the plank extended from the massive alien vessel resembling a vampire squid.

## What's in a Name?

"You have Hanson's Disease, Mr. Barker."

"Whew! Well, I didn't think my dry eyes and skin irritation would amount to anything serious."

"The more common term for what you have is leprosy," clarified the doctor.

## Downsizing

Braker, as he was called, jumped into his supercharged Studebaker Golden Hawk and roared toward the cliff's edge. Everybody watched to see if he'd break his old record in which he'd stopped just 18 inches shy of the 425-foot drop-off to the canyon floor. "Go, Braker … go!" shouted the three members of his pit crew. Their cheers quickly turned to silence when the dust cleared and their ace driver's vehicle was nowhere to be seen. "Shoot!" they grumbled, "All we got left now is the damn Lark."

# Adjusting One's Priorities

Frank saw a small plane flip and fall to earth. He had five minutes left of his lunch hour and still had not eaten his dessert. *What should I do?* he wondered.

*Michael C. Keith*

## IT IS SAID WE HAVE MORE IN COMMON THAN WE DO OUR DIFFERENCES

Zeooope took a long, hard look from the window of the spaceship as it neared the bluest planet he'd ever seen. *Maybe this will make a good home as long as we remain at a safe distance from the liquid that covers nearly all of the surface,* he thought. *It has everything else we need to sustain our existence.* When the craft touched down on the remote plains of eastern Wyoming, the aliens hastily burrowed into the ground, hiding any trace of their existence. It would only be in the deepest cover of night that they would resurface to conduct their first rock/paper/scissors competition since leaving their home constellation.

## Sometimes It Takes …

Nothing manages to shake me from my deep funk until I see a photograph in the Travel section of the Sunday *New York Times* of a Tibetan woman breastfeeding a yak.

*Michael C. Keith*

## You Bet Your Life

Six old friends got together and decided to wager on whom among them would live the longest. Each would put five dollars into the hat each week, and the last person standing would win. Since they all were only in their early 70s, they felt the pot could end up being quite substantial, and that's what spurred them on—that and the fact that each septuagenarian felt he was in better shape than the others. The first member of the group passed away after five years, and over the next dozen years, everyone else in the pool had expired, except one. Unfortunately, he could neither stand up nor recall anything about the bet.

## Go Fuck Yourself, Cuz!

I'd like to be less significant to those who love me, because I don't want them to be pained by my passing. The idea upsets me. So I've figured out what to do to prevent this from happening. I will be a prick to all of them from now until I die.

*Michael C. Keith*

## WHEN REPRISAL BACKFIRES AND YOU LOOK THE FOOL AGAIN

Marvin kept telling his wife that her favorite stars had died even though they hadn't. He loved to see her over-the-top reaction to his fake news. After being duped a half-dozen times, she decided to turn the tables on him and falsely report that one of his favorite celebrities on *The Lawrence Welk Show* had died. The joke was on her, however, because Myron Floren had passed away the year before.

# Irresponsible Parenting

On the news, there's a story about a magnetic tic-tac-toe game being recalled because the magnets might fall off and kids could eat them. I want to know what kind of parents would let their kids eat magnets. And then I think, of course—parents who have kids with iron deficiencies.

*Michael C. Keith*

# WHEN AN APPROPRIATE LEVEL OF SYMPATHY GOES MISSING

Tim was reading a story in an old issue of *The New Yorker*. It really grabbed him. *So beautifully written, and way beyond anything I'm capable of doing,* he told himself. After he finished the piece, he Googled its author and discovered he'd died in an accident only two days after receiving the coveted National Short Fiction Prize. It struck Tim as a damn pity the award had been given to someone who'd made such limited use of it.

## So Close but Yet ...

A young hitchhiker with a giant backpack flung over his left shoulder stood at the entrance to the highway on-ramp. As I watched him from inside the garage that was fixing my flat, I couldn't help think he was lacking something in the common-sense department. To stand where he was deprived him of all the potential rides up on the interstate. All he had to do was walk another 80 feet and he'd improve his chances a hundredfold. Furthermore, it struck me as foolish to be holding the monster backpack rather than just putting it on the ground until a ride came along. The hitchhiker had yet to secure a lift by the time my repair was made, so I figured I'd pick him up. I wasn't sure where he was headed, but the idea of someone to talk with during the 300 miles I had left on my trip was appealing. I stopped just beyond where he stood and waved him over. He stuck his head into the passenger-side window and asked where I was going. "To St. Louis," I answered, opening the door to let him in. "Oh, no thanks," he replied, backing away. "I'm going to *East* St. Louis."

*Michael C. Keith*

# Self-Immolation

After looking through it dozens of times, Janice can't decide if the book she's written was worth her effort or deserves the public's attention. Some things in it stand up to her scrutiny, but other things don't. As weeks go by, the latter view begins to outweigh the former, and then she's finally at the point where nothing in her book seems worthy of the paper and ink used to publish it.

# Postmortem Fetal Extrusion

Cynthia Morton was the result of a coffin birth—a non-technical term pertaining to child delivery while deceased. Eight months pregnant, the elder Morton had suddenly collapsed and died. The built-up gases in her body caused her fetus to be expelled as she lay in the woods days before being noticed by a passing jogger. It was a fact first revealed to Cynthia by her family's physician and friend when she was 16. "The fetuses are always nonviable ... except in your case," he had said, adding, "You were one for the record books. An amazing survival." The information had haunted her through the balance of her adolescence. The thought that she'd emerged into the world from a decomposing corpse never failed to make her feel queasy and strange. Then, on the occasion of her 21st birthday, she was provided by the doctor with additional facts, which removed the stigma of her bizarre birth. "Your delivery is possibly attributable to your mother having consumed a large bean enchilada immediately following her participation in a junior Iron Man competition." Cynthia didn't know why it helped knowing that; it just did.

Michael C. Keith

## Sometimes a Little Compromise Is All It Takes

Marvin grew Saltillo primrose, trailing acacia, and tufted evening primrose in front of his adobe-style house in Milton, Massachusetts. The architecture and landscaping of his property upset his neighbors, who took great pride in their traditional Capes and Colonials, accented by *Hydrangea paniculata, Spiraea nipponica,* and a variety of other local flora and fauna. "You've violated the integrity of our quaint settlement," complained the Hancocks and Porters. "This is *not* New Mexico, you know!" groused the Johnsons and Taylors. Taking their concern to heart, Marvin installed a flagpole with a New England Patriots banner on his front lawn. "Well, that does the trick," said the Hancocks and Porters. "Yes, that makes a huge difference," observed the Johnsons and Taylors.

# Obit

Forty-seven-year-old Harvey Samson lost his fight with cancer on October 16. His assailant remains at large.

*Michael C. Keith*

## When Things Don't Add Up

His death was totally unexpected the second time. He was supposed to die from pancreatic cancer but had managed to survive it against all odds. His end coming as it did while running the Boston Marathon was a shock to everyone. He was the picture of fitness and had been training for the event since his remission two years earlier. All anyone could think was some kind of macabre joke of fate had killed him. Who wouldn't believe that when someone slips to death on an orange peel? Of course, the thing that really added to the bizarre nature of the fatal accident was the fact that he was an executive at Minute Maid.

## Fuck Them!

There was no place to sit. I had boarded the spacecraft at the alien's invitation and then found there was no goddamn chair on which to take the load off. Immediately I decided that this was a foreign species I wanted no part of if it couldn't even provide for the most basic of human needs.

## End Date

Is it time to call it quits? Stop these dark thoughts about death and dying. Why not? I've only got a few more years left anyway, and this is no way to spend them. Yeah, it's the sensible thing to do. Take those pills I've stockpiled. Get out of this torment. When should I do it? Probably after next week's birthday party for our grandson. That should be fun. He's such a sweet kid. The following week is the play I've been so eager to catch. Rave reviews. Well, let's see. Oh, there's the trip to the lake on the 29$^{th}$ and 30$^{th}$ we've been looking forward to all year. Wouldn't want to miss it. Next month is booked solid with things, too. Shit, this is going to be a problem.

# Foe

What do I do with this unmitigable fear of the end? I'd like to knock it down and stamp on it ... eradicate it. But it hovers out of reach in its dark, ruthless majesty.

# Scent

Alice Hampton stood at the kitchen window and watched as her 10-year-old son played catch with his friends. It was an image from years earlier when baseball had been his first love. When he reached his teens, music became the center of his world. No longer did he play ball with the neighborhood kids in the yard. Now he shut himself away in his room, rarely making an appearance, even during key family activities.

Alice's husband, Josh, attempted to allay his wife's concerns about her son's growing anti-social behavior by claiming he'd done the same when he was that age.

"Nothing as weird as adolescent boys. Believe me, I can attest to that. I was a hermit until I left for college. Think my parents forgot what I looked like."

Nevertheless, Alice insisted her son go to counseling, which he had until his suicide. Immediately following the 15-year-old's death, she'd sealed off his room and forbade anyone from entering it. She was determined to preserve his smell. It was in it that she found solace when the pain of his absence became too much for her to bear.

"We should clear out his stuff and open up the room. We can't keep it as a tomb. It just makes things worse for everyone. A constant reminder of what happened," argued Josh, but it was to no avail, because Alice believed as long as she could take in her late child's lingering fragrance, he would remain alive to her.

The Hamptons' existence took another dramatic turn when they returned home from a visit to Josh's ailing mother. As soon as their car entered the driveway, Alice noticed that the window to her son's bedroom had been shattered. She let out a deep moan and leapt from the car. When she reached her dead son's room, she spotted the source of the intrusion—a baseball on the floor in the middle of a pile of broken glass. "Oh, no!" she wailed, sniffing hard at the air that flowed out of the open window. "He's gone ... my baby is *gone!*"

*Michael C. Keith*

## From That Moment On

Dr. Wayne Dyer, the self-development guru, jogged past Ryan as he sat on the beach in Ft. Lauderdale. It was shortly after Ryan had read *Your Erroneous Zones,* Dyer's monster bestseller. The book had greatly moved Ryan, and he took the sighting of the author as a significant sign—a validation of everything the volume espoused. Yes ... oh, yes; he was going to *create* himself.

# Old Clip on YouTube

I watch a man in a fedora and zoot suit walking down Lexington Avenue in 1948. *Who was he?* I wonder, and think, *that's me being watched by a stranger in Iowa 50 years from now, when I'm dead, too.*

*Michael C. Keith*

## Temporary Measures

The problem with the septic tank kept Tim awake. It had for three straight nights. The pump guy had said it wasn't leaching properly and would likely need some expensive repairs. "What if we reduce our use of it," Tim had asked, to which the pump guy had responded, "If you shit half as much, in its current condition it will last twice as long before you need to fix it."

# On Possessing a Belief in the Secret Powers of Friends

Leonard wrote a letter to everyone he knew intended to be read after he died. It said, "I don't want to be here, and if you can do something to bring me back, please do."

*Michael C. Keith*

# A Process of Elimination

Foley, Idaho, stood on a small rise against an outcropping of huge boulders known as The Giants. It was almost an ideal place to live. What kept it from being ideal was the fact that a murderer lived among its residents. Three people had been killed so far, and the sheriff had no suspects. Everybody was on edge and in a dark mood, anticipating the next homicide. When a fourth person was found dead, a dozen townsfolk decided to take matters into their own hands. They armed themselves and set about the task of eliminating who they felt was the most likely suspect. In quick order they had executed several people. A month passed without incident, and the group felt it had achieved its goal. But then another person was discovered murdered. The self-appointed enforcers then executed a half dozen more individuals they believed might be the killer. Again, a month went by with no further homicides, but then a sixth victim was found. The vigilantes set to work once more, this time shooting half of the town's citizens. However, after this round of mass slayings they felt they should do more to ensure the murderer was removed once and for all. With this in mind, they shot all of the community's remaining occupants. Convinced that they had finally achieved the result they had sought, the twelve vigilantes gathered in the town square to celebrate. There, eleven of them were shot dead by a member of their posse.

# Degrading: Attack au Fer

Hours into his end-of-semester grading marathon, the instructor of Renaissance history came across a sentence in one of his term papers that startled him and impelled him to act. It read, "I am standing behind you with my rapier in first position." Norman spun around in his swivel chair, his two feet together at the heel and his dominant hand prepared to parry. He then realized he had no foil either in his fist or in the room.

Michael C. Keith

# ON DEFERRING A DECISION IN THE FACE OF LIKELY ANNIHILATION

My next-door neighbor called me in the middle of the night to report that a wall of missiles armed with nuclear warheads was heading across the Pacific in our direction. "I don't know to what extent we should be concerned about it," he added, "but I thought you may want to take appropriate action." After mulling his words, I asked what he felt might be *appropriate action* in this situation. He paused before replying and then suggested we take up the subject again in the morning when we were thinking more clearly. As I was about to say goodbye, he inquired about the block party planned for the following week. It led to further conversation.

## One Must Expect Change

While Fred sat in his reading chair, he heard a trickling sound behind him. When he turned to check it out, an enormous gush of water struck him. *It was just a trickle when I first heard it,* he thought, quite surprised.

*Michael C. Keith*

# Small but Meaningful Consolation

On his best days, 19-year-old Jacob could run from Wallace to Sharon Springs, Kansas, and back and barely break a sweat. It was a marathon run, he told himself, and one day he'd go to Boston and run in their famous race. Maybe not win it, but surely make a good showing. The problem facing him was getting enough money together to make the trip to the New England city. He'd saved half the cost of the bus ticket, but getting the fare for the ride back home had been a problem. Finally, after many lean years, the family's farm was having an exceptional harvest, and it looked as if Jacob might finally be able to realize his dream. His parents knew what he'd wanted to do and had encouraged him to keep training, even though they'd only been partially able to help him. Now they were thinking they could do more. "If things keep going like they are, we'll get you that ticket, son." Then the flex auger head on their ancient combine gave out, and they had to reevaluate their situation. "Maybe we'll get you that ticket next year, Jacob, but we got to get this old thing fixed or we'll have trouble just paying for basics," said his father. It left Jacob feeling bereft, and he stopped running. This pained his parents, and nothing they could say got him back out on US 40. As the years passed, Jacob fell out of shape, and then, at 31, he developed a brain aneurism and died. His parents figured if he'd continued to run, he would have lived. They were plagued by guilt. However, Jacob's doctor observed that their son could well have died sooner, because the physical stress from long-distance running would likely have hastened his demise. "Well, then it's a good thing we never got him that return ticket," observed Jacob's father, feeling a little better about the whole thing.

## Farewell Soirée

Everybody said it was the most pleasant wake they'd ever attended. A local French restaurant noted for its fine four-star cuisine had catered it. Tuxedoed servers kept long-stemmed flutes filled with champagne and silver platters with crab and caviar brioche circulating. Especially impressive were the lavish flower arrangements—no lilies or carnations but instead magnificent rare orchids adorned the elegant banquet room. In addition, rather than prerecorded music typical of such somber occasions, a string quartet performed a medley of light classical compositions. Not an hour into the affair attendees were told it was time to hide because the newly engaged couple was about to arrive for their surprise reception.

Michael C. Keith

# When It Appears You've Been Blessed with Good Fortune but You're Mistaken

On the TGV from Prague to Vienna, Ambroz Kozisek fell ill. He thought it was the pork dumplings he'd eaten at a Nadrazi Depot kiosk before boarding. *Foolish to eat such things, and so quickly,* he chided himself.

An hour after departure, the pain in his abdomen had reached such a point that he asked a fellow passenger to fetch the conductor.

"We shall reach Jihlava shortly, *mein Herr.* Are you able to make it? If not, I shall see if there's a doctor on board."

Ambroz thought about it for a moment and concluded he needed immediate medical attention.

"Please, get me help now," he beseeched the train master.

Soon a young physician appeared on the scene.

"What are your symptoms, sir?" he inquired.

"Very bad belly ache," moaned Ambroz.

"Sorry," said the doctor, turning to leave. "My specialty is feet."

## *You Can't Go Home Again*

When his wife of 47 years died, Albert retired from his job, sold his house in a suburb of Baltimore, and moved back to his birthplace in northern Minnesota. It pleased him that the town looked the same as it had when he'd left it 50 years before. Adding to his satisfaction, he found that many of his childhood friends still lived there, but when he tried to have a conversation with them, he discovered they spoke a foreign language.

Michael C. Keith

# When the Dead Speak, They May Say Something You Don't Want to Hear

The Old Colony Cemetery rose a couple hundred feet above the single-lane blacktop that ran between Carlton and Jefferstown. Because of its steep angle, many of the headstones leaned forward creating the unsettling sense that corpses were about to descend onto passersby. Those who traveled the stretch often claimed to hear voices emanating from the boxes in the hill. Eventually their testimonies came to the attention of Bernard Lansky, an amateur paranormal investigator and assistant professor of child studies at a junior college in the next county.

The academic set out to corroborate the reports on his newly purchased Spirit Box SB11. Indeed, he'd tried to record hauntings at other locations but had met with no success. But this time his confidence of capturing the sounds of the netherworld was very high given the vast number of claims from the gravesite. *This will be an enormous accomplishment. It will put me on the map,* thought Bernard, imagining his photo on the front page of major publications and on screens around the globe.

On a bright Sunday morning, he set up his audio device and sat under a rheumy oak tree while it transcribed ambient sounds. All that Bernard heard—passing cars, chirping birds, engines of passing jets—was caught by the recorder, but there were no spectral utterances. Undeterred, he returned to the cemetery many times over the next few weeks.

Then it happened—voices from beneath the field of tilting monuments. He couldn't make out what they were saying until he played them back on his duplicating machine. What he heard both amazed and and upset him. "Bernard is a pedophile!" chimed an ethereal chorus, over and over again.

It was not something he felt he could reveal to the world.

*Michael C. Keith*

## WHEN PETS SURPRISE YOU

Twenty-seven black-capped chickadees were found dead in the courtyard of the duke's palace. Given the condition of their bodies, it was concluded they had died simultaneously. This baffled investigators—until they deduced that the house cat was a sorcerer.

# NASA Retrieves a Message from an Extraterrestrial Object

"You humans are among the most insignificant life forms in the universe. Yet you cling to the misguided notion there's something left for you after you expire. Your dull intelligences are of no value to any of the more evolved organisms that exist beyond your barren orb."

## AWARENESS

Professor Frey was losing confidence in his ability to give a coherent lecture. For nearly 40 years, he'd been conveying the same body of information, but now he found its central points and details eluded him, leaving him to grasp for something to fill the awkward gaps.

Finally, he so feared going completely blank in the classroom that he began to cancel sessions. After countless absences, he decided to come clean to his longtime boss, Dr. Sanders. He called the department chair, saying that conducting classes had become a major problem, promising to explain why, if they could meet.

"Well, can you give me a vague idea what's going on?" asked Sanders.

After a prolonged pause, Frey replied, "Why did you call me?"

# In the Order of Importance

Sylvia Blumenthal is on her way home from the milliners. She stands at the corner of 14th Street and 8th Avenue waiting to cross the busy thoroughfare. When the light turns signaling cars to stop for pedestrians, she steps from the curb. It's the last thing she remembers before being told her left leg below the knee had to be amputated because of the accident. "Where's my new hat?" she asks. "I can't have lost my new hat."

Michael C. Keith

## WHAT YOU DON'T HAVE ...

There was a planet that had never known violence or unhappiness. It had experienced complete tranquility since its origin. More than anything it wanted to know despair. Its curiosity ultimately proved a problem.

# Putting Up with the Inconveniences of a Paradise

As Herbert was about to climb into the shower, two scorpions climbed from the drain. He leapt back in horror and let out a shriek. *This place will kill me yet,* he thought, recalling the events of the day. In the morning, on the way to where he was meeting with a group of NGOs, the vehicle in which he was a passenger inexplicably caught fire. Then a large venomous snake was curled up on the counter of the lunchroom when he and his colleagues filed in. It was brushed away by a worker, and where it went was unknown. Herbert had spent his meal with one eye on the floor, in the event the reptile reappeared. Topping off the day, on the return ride to his hotel, his party encountered an agitated elephant that threatened to trample them. *Christ! Will I survive this trip?* he grumbled, turning on the showerhead, hoping to chase away the arachnids. However, the feeble spray was hardly enough to disrupt their climb over the ledge that led out of the stall. "Goddamn!" bellowed Herbert, grabbing his boot and stomping the life out of the critters. In the days leading up to his departure from Tanzania, he would experience a host of other near disasters. While he waited to board his flight at the airport in Dar es Salaam, he sat on a wobbly wooden bench and sipped a tepid cup of coffee and munched on a stale chunk of fried dough that attracted a swarm of hungry black flies. *I'll miss this country,* he thought, recalling the magnificent Ngorongoro Crater, Serengeti Desert, and Mount Kilimanjaro.

*Michael C. Keith*

## SILVER LINING

Babies were being born without eyes but retained the ability to see. At first this was very disconcerting to parents, but then they came to think of it as a blessing because of the elimination of chronic blepharitis.

# Frontier Justice

Buffalo Bill Cody took great pride in having scalped a young Cheyenne warrior named Yellow Hair. It came shortly after his good friend Colonel Armstrong Custer had been killed at Little Big Horn, and the gruesome act appeased his need for revenge. Over time, thanks mainly to Cody's exploitation of the event in his Wild West extravaganzas, it became a part of the showman's legend. In old age, suffering from kidney failure, Cody claimed he saw the ghost of Yellow Hair, who he believed was intent on cutting off his famous locks in retaliation for what he'd suffered. Ever the strategist, Cody wore a wig over his hair in order to fool his irate pursuer and preserve his scalp. The plan succeeded, as the apparition ripped the wig from his head and quickly vanished with it. However, in the specter's place appeared a vast herd of buffalo, which the fabled hunter alleged were out to even the score for the atrocities he'd committed against them. While Cody's widow could tolerate the presence of a vindictive ghoul, she could not abide the endless trail of dung the vengeful beasts left behind.

*Michael C. Keith*

## An Unsettling Comment

We're all shooting the shit and sucking up what's at least our third beer, when out of the blue Craig says, "I'm grieving all the time because my imagination constantly defaults to tragedy. Christ, I don't know how many times I've witnessed you guys dying."

## Sometimes Something Opens a Door Long Closed

"If you're a sixty- or seventy-year-old man, you likely have clogged arteries or the beginning of them," said Lyle's primary-care physician after his examination. "So we'll have you checked out, and if you have an obstruction, which your symptoms sort of indicate, we'll have it taken care of. This kind of open-heart surgery is fairly routine these days, but not entirely without risks." Lyle returned home and accessed the file of the book he'd been working on for several years. He found he was no longer blocked.

Michael C. Keith

# MESSAGE TO EARTH BY SUSTENANCE HARVESTERS FROM ANOTHER WORLD

*We will discard your consciousness because it is of no value to us. But we will use your body parts. On our planet, nutritious food is in very short supply. We appreciate your understanding. Our ETA is tomorrow.*

## Coping Behavior

So I get this email telling me a colleague of mine had a heart attack and is in the hospital ICU awaiting quadruple bypass surgery. That evening my wife and I go to a movie, and we spot his wife in the ticket line. She doesn't see us, and we don't go in. "What the hell is she doing going to a movie the day her husband almost dies of a heart attack?" I ask my wife. She says maybe she needed some distraction. I say, "What, your spouse having a coronary isn't enough distraction?" She replies, "No, I mean from the shock of his having a one. Probably needed to get her mind off it." "So if he *dies,* she's going on holiday?" I respond.

*Michael C. Keith*

## Two-O'Clock Jump

Harry James's boys climbed onto the bus for their next gig in Cincinnati. Marty Kline, one of the band's two trombonists, was feeling punk. He hadn't moved his bowels in over a week. An hour into the ride from Cleveland, they let loose. But the musician was unaware of this because he was fast asleep. His seatmate leapt up as the spillage from Marty's lower region trickled against his leg. "Jesus Christ, he's shitting all over me!" he bellowed, rousing everyone on the bus and prompting the band's leader to grab his baton and start conducting.

# Doubt Is the Enemy of Creativity*

As I sit down to continue my tale about a blind three-legged zebra that wanders into the Yaya Shopping Centre in Nairobi, I scan the rows of novels on my shelves and wonder if what I'm writing is worth my time.

*Observed Sylvia Plath.

Michael C. Keith

## Dreams Can Be Just That

We'd spend hours at the top of Bailey's Bluff talking about what we were going to do when we grew up. The endless view up there filled us with a huge sense of possibility about our futures. We would reach beyond the horizon and accomplish great things. In my mind, I exceeded my friend's ambitions. While they were content to become captains of industry, I planned to become President of the United States. Fifty years later, the three of us retired from the Western Nebraska Sugar Beet Cooperative in Minatare. For the most part, we were okay with where our lives had taken us.

## Pre-emptive Strike

The chemo waiting room was crowded. Patients nodded at one another like soldiers about to enter combat.

*Michael C. Keith*

## Encounter with a Stranger in a Big City

I was looking out of my hotel room on the eighth floor when I saw a naked woman standing in a window across the street. She was not aware of me, and I couldn't stop looking at her exposed body. Then she spotted me and quickly drew her curtains. I felt guilty for gaping at her and closed my shades as well. For a while I wondered who she was and why she was standing there nude. The next morning, I saw the same woman in her window, but this time she was fully clothed ... and I was not.

# GRATITUDE

Mama Loti serve da rice from da big black pot. She give me extra 'cause she like me best of all. Da other kids dey get mad 'cause she do that but dey don't say nothin' 'cause she keep the rice from dem if dey do. Guess Mama Loti think I be smarter than the rest, and I be dat ... stronger, too. Maybe 'cause I be older and bigger, she like me more. I think she okay, but when I grow one mo' year, I gonna take over dat pot of rice, even I got to do mean to her. She be easy to put down 'cause she slow and fat. Other boys not say nothin' 'cause they be 'fraid. Den I give out da rice, but no extra to the biggest and smartest boy so he don't do me like I do Mama Loti.

# Hermantage

From his two-room dwelling on the high plains of Kansas, Herman could see the faint rise of the Rockies on the western horizon. In all other directions, his view was unobstructed by objects either formed by nature or man. If you looked closely, there was a curve to the earth all around him. He'd written that to his sister, Nell, back in West Virginia. Adding that he was over three thousand feet above sea level without any sign of how it got to be so far up. She was intrigued by what he'd told her, but never enough to make the 1,200-mile trip to see it for herself. That was fine by him, because he preferred his solitude. It was his thinking that when you got people around you your life got messy.

# Disregarding Bad News

When it was clear the asteroid was about to strike Earth, thus annihilating all living things, Sam told his son he could use the family car as long as he brought it home with a full tank.

*Michael C. Keith*

## Everyone Has a Price

"If Muleton could boast of anything it would be that it has the most boarded-up stores in Texas ... maybe the whole country," said Don Parsons.

"So you're proposing we close down the ones that are still open and turn the place into a ghost town theme park?" asked the town manager, Hank Savoy.

"Hell, it's already a ghost town, so we may as well make it official. The place is on its last leg."

"Well, you got a point about that, but I don't think you'll get Vernon and Carl to go out of business to make room for your scheme, even if it does have some merit."

"So I'll ask them."

"What do you think, Manny and Clyde? You go along with this?" asked Hank."

Muleton's two remaining selectmen mumbled something to each other and then spoke.

"Place is on life-support anyway, so what've we got to lose?" said Clyde.

"Fine with me. I'm moving away in June. Good luck with this," added Manny.

Don left Savoy's double-wide to pursue his plan. Vernon agreed to shut his doors, indicating he'd been intending to do so for a while. However, Carl was strongly against the idea.

"Hell no! I'm not closing down. This business has been in my family for over 70 years. I still have enough customers to pay my bills. What else am I going to do? No way your harebrained idea is going to keep us all from starving."

Since Carl's store occupied the greatest amount of square footage on Muleton's main street, the plan to convert the hamlet into a tourist attraction seemed in jeopardy. Then Don came up with a ruse he thought might change his opponent's mind … and he was right.

"If you don't go along with this, we'll kill your wife. We can make that happen, you know."

"Really…? Well, if you do that, you've got a deal," replied Carl.

*Michael C. Keith*

## LOST IN SPACE

Aidan's new girlfriend made a statement that puzzled everyone in the room. Said she, "I'm so far away from perfection as a human being the James Webb Space Telescope will never locate me." Nobody had any idea what the fuck the James Webb Space Telescope was.

## Variation

The camera pans down the side of the Woolworth Building in the 1948 documentary. A single camouflaged vehicle moves slowly up Broadway, a gun turret on its roof. The sidewalks are empty as the narrator proclaims, "RESISTANCE IS FUTILE." A Nazi flag flaps in the breeze above the entrance to 233.

*Michael C. Keith*

## "One Good Deed Is Not Enough to Redeem a Man from a Lifetime of Wickedness"

It's the general consensus that Buddy Cianci transformed the city of Providence when he was mayor. What used to be a dismal New England mill town became a radiant metropolitan center lauded by the national media. Cianci went to prison for unethical practices while holding office. His supporters, and they were legion, felt he should have been allowed a few transgressions, given all the good he did.

## "Where you going?" asked the driver to the hitchhiker.

"That way," responded the old man, nodding in the direction the pickup was pointed. By noon the next day, they were there.

*Michael C. Keith*

## Henry Had Ambitions Thwarted by the Effects of Time

"Bought a Blue Midnight Hohner mouth organ. Decent mid-price blues harp. Always wanted to learn an instrument and figured it would give me something to do into retirement. That was a while back. Well, almost two years ago. Problem now is my arthritis makes it hard to hold the damn thing, so I bought one of those neck-holder doodads like Dylan and Young use. Worked for a while; now my upper plate keeps coming loose even though I use that Poly Grip stuff. Got about two-thirds of the way through learning "Amazing Grace," to about where the choir—if there was a choir—would be singing: 'And grace will lead us home.' Then had to give up on it. Maybe there's something I can play with my feet … while they still work."

Let Us Now Speak of Extinction

# Why Frank Failed as a Creator of Word Puzzles

He worked in a hardware store for 28 years. Married his high-school sweetheart. Belonged to the choir at his church. Owned two all-terrain vehicles. Suffered from chronic lower back pain. What color were his eyes? *


* Rejected by *Variety Puzzles Magazine* for failure to provide sufficient information leading to an appropriate answer.

*Michael C. Keith*

## Authorities in New Dawn, Vermont, Break with Procedure

He claimed he was innocent and didn't waver from that position. When the police found him just blocks from the scene of the murder, he was covered in blood and had a knife in his hand that was later determined to be the murder weapon. The gore found on his clothes matched that on the body and witnesses claimed they'd seen him attack the victim. Furthermore, motive was established, since he and the dead woman had been estranged and a restraining order had been issued against the suspect because of threats he'd made to her. All this was consistent with charges listed on his long rap sheet that included two previous assaults on women he'd been associated with. For two days the police interrogated him, but he wouldn't admit to the homicide. Impressed by his resolve to stick with his story, they decided to set him free, telling him to have a nice day.

## INSOMNIA

He can't get to sleep because he keeps thinking it's a dress rehearsal for death. Finally, he succumbs, and, in his dream, he's debating the existence of God with his friend. "This business of an afterlife is foolish," he declares. And then he wakes up ... grateful that he has.

## Price Over Prejudice

To Henry White, there was a terrorist under every bed and around every corner. When his wife suggested they go on vacation to France, he balked, claiming it would be tantamount to committing suicide.

"Those crazy Arabs are shooting and blowing up everything over there," he growled.

When she countered by recommending they take a road trip in the U.S., he claimed it was also a major risk, given how foreigners, namely Muslims, had infiltrated every sector of the country.

"Well, then, where the heck can we go?" she complained.

Her husband thought about it for a while and then proposed a staycation. After much back and forth, Mrs. Beaumont agreed to her husband's idea if he would build them an elaborate lanai and install an Olympic-size pool.

"Are you crazy? You know how much that would cost?" he protested.

"Well, then we're going on a trip," she responded.

The following week Henry hired the Ahmed Yusuf Ali Home Improvement Company because of its reasonable rates.

# Wake Up, for Christ's Sake!

The sun is rising, but it shouldn't be. It's 2 a.m., and I'm not in the Arctic Circle, where that may be normal. It's Kansas City, and there's real confusion and anxiety here about the premature dawn. The TV news says the National Weather Service is looking into it, but this is above their pay grade. It should have the White House's attention, but apparently the President is still asleep.

*Michael C. Keith*

## HE DIED WHILE SHE WAS GONE

She'd planned her trip to visit her cousin in Italy two years in advance. Her husband decided not to accompany her, since he felt his wife would enjoy exclusive time with her last remaining relative in the country she was born in. At first his wife was okay with going without him, but as the trip neared, she became anxious because of her spouse's heart trouble. "Don't worry about me. I'll be just fine," he'd assured her.

# Bad Chemistry

My friend was planning to give away her Chemcraft Atomic Energy Chemistry Set. She said she didn't want it anymore, but I wanted it really bad and tried to convince her that I was the best kid to give it to. Unfortunately, she had the idea that giving it to Goodwill was the better thing to do—a more legitimate act of charity. She said she thought it didn't count as a good deed if she gave it to me. So, I was out of luck and deeply disappointed. When I realized it was a waste of time to plead for it any further, I said I wouldn't be her friend anymore. In fact, I told her if she did give it to me, I would use it to blow up her house.

*Michael C. Keith*

## MOTIVES CAN BE DIFFICULT TO FATHOM

A charm of hummingbirds alighted from the church belfry and poked at the reverend's head with their invisible tongues until he relented and dropped his Bible.

## Animus

"Just don't let your dog shit on my lawn. That's all I ask," said the man, as Gary walked by.

It pissed him off that the stranger would assume his dog had been relieving itself on his property, especially since his dog never went to the bathroom while on a leash.

"My dog doesn't do that. He only goes in his own yard," said Gary.

"Well, I just don't want animals crapping on my lawn. They kill it, and I spend a lot of money keeping it up."

Gary thought about letting the whole thing drop, but the man's surly attitude got to him.

"As you can see, I'm walking my dog in the street, not on your lawn, mister. So save your words for someone who's letting their dog dump on your precious grass."

"Animals shit where they want, and people don't control them."

"This dog owner does, and I don't appreciate your accusing me of doing otherwise."

The two men gave each other a hard look, and then went about their business—Gary doing his on the man's lawn.

Michael C. Keith

# Is More Information Necessary?

He was born on September 11, 2001, and his mother said it was the most wonderful day there ever was.

## Feel the Beat

*Sixty to seventy beats a minute is normal, so 80 beats isn't bad,* thought Shirley, her ear pressed against her pillow. She tried adjusting her heart rate but to no avail. In fact, it sped up and this frightened her. In the past, she'd had impressive success lowering the number of times her heart moved but never before had she experienced a rise in its pace. She climbed from bed in a panic and stood in the darkness with her fingers pressed against her neck. "It's not going down ... getting faster," she whimpered. *The Metoprolol. Take one. Slow this down before you have a heart attack.* Shirley dashed to the bathroom, nearly falling over her sleeping dog. As usual, she had trouble removing the cap from the pill bottle, and it didn't help that her hand was shaking badly. Once the vial was open, she put it to her lips and swallowed several of the small white tablets. When she realized what she'd done, she tried to vomit the meds but could not bring them up. "Oh, my God, what's going to happen to me?" she moaned, continuing to poke her fingers down her throat, her nails drawing blood. Finally, she managed to heave the clump of pills into the sink. Gasping and staring at her frazzled image in the medicine cabinet mirror, she began to weep. "You're pathetic," she mumbled and took her pulse again. A smile replaced her tears. "Thank you ... *thank you,* 70 beats! You're normal again, old girl." Rather than return to bed, Shirley went to the kitchen. After all of the frenzy, she'd developed a substantial appetite. A tremendous urge for banana chocolate chip waffles and coffee ... lots of coffee.

Michael C. Keith

## COTILLION OF THE FITTEST

It wasn't three days after the last human died that the cockroaches and rats held a dance.

# When the Right Thing to Do Doesn't Seem Quite Right

My friend, Celia, and I were walking through Montgomery Ward on Harris Avenue because we had nothing better to do, since there was no school. Although she didn't have any money, Celia decided to try on a skirt she liked. A few minutes later she came out of the dressing room with a funny look on her face.

"What?" I asked, and she signaled for me to follow her as she quickly moved toward the store's exit.

When we were outside, I asked her what was up, and she took out a wallet from inside her jacket.

"Where'd you get that? I asked, knowing it wasn't hers, and she said she found it on the floor of the changing stall she was in.

"Someone must have dropped it. Let's see what's in it," she said excitedly.

"Better take it back," I said, as she opened the wallet.

"Holy cow, bet there's 10 bucks in it," she squealed.

"Ten bucks?" I blurted, and she turned and took off down the street, signaling for me to follow.

When we were a couple of blocks away, I asked if she was keeping it, and she said yes,

"But it's probably got all the person's important stuff in it ... license and things," I protested.

"You get half the money because you were with me when I found it."

"Really ... *half?*"

"Still want me to take it back?" she asked.

Minutes later we were ordering grilled frankfurters and grape sodas at HoJos.

## Global Scourge

"The deadly pandemic is approaching Old Crow," claimed the local newsletter, so Garth went deep into the tundra, carrying with him what he believed were enough supplies to help him survive until he could make it on his own. However, what he'd taken with him ran out sooner than he expected, so he was forced to return to his village to gather more provisions. When he reached the main road, he was shaken to find a just-built McDonalds. *Yes,* he thought, *the plague has reached us.*

*Michael C. Keith*

# How Atheism Flourished in Modern Times

He wanted so much to come back and tell everyone there really was life after death. But then he was told to keep them guessing.

# A Happy Realization

He frets because he can't find a match to ignite when the room fills up with gas from the stove. It upsets his plan to blow himself up. Then it occurs to him if he remains in the room while it fills up with gas, he won't need a match to do the job.

*Michael C. Keith*

## One Good Deed …

Thirty-one *croque-monsieurs* were delivered to 78 Rue Avidité in the 18th District. When the bearer said they were already paid for, even the gratuity, Zidane broke into tears. He had never experienced such kindness in his long life. Now the question he faced was how to conceal the sandwiches from the other thirty men in the building so they would not eat them before he could.

## What the Minister Said That Disturbed His Congregation

"There are only horrors waiting us in the future."

## Coming to Terms

"You take 10 pills a day to keep going in old age, but that chemistry accrues in your body and gives you other maladies that require additional prescriptions. Soon you're ingesting enough medicine to deepen the profits of the pharmaceutical industry," observed 91-year-old Roy Windom.

"True, it's a vicious cycle, but I guess we're lucky we have stuff that protects us," replied 89-year-old Mildred Connors.

The waitress placed a check on the table and asked the elderly couple if they'd like more coffee.

"Guess life would be pretty miserable without all those prophylactics," offered Roy, taking a five-dollar bill from his wallet.

"You said it. There's no way I'd want to get pregnant," said Mildred, attempting to extricate herself from the restaurant booth.

# CANINE I.Q.

She knows she can't fly, so when birds taunt her from the trees, she ignores them.

## SEQUEL

Riley had written an account of his unusual childhood working in the circus with his bearded mother, and it had been published. Reviewers had been kind, and he felt gratified that his story had been told and well received. As he approached retirement age, it occurred to him to write another memoir, this one about his adult years. After a careful inventory of his post-adolescent existence (his first reminiscence had ended when he was 18), he felt he had some pretty solid material. He proposed the idea to his publisher, who after reviewing it encouraged him to go forward with the autobiography but suggested he write it as a novel. "You mean fictionalize my life?" he asked, perplexed. After a thoughtful moment, the publisher replied, "I think after 45 years as a parking garage attendant you might be wise to do that."

## Time Is a Joy-Killer

I look for my name on the winner's list. It's not there. The following year I look again. It's still not there. This happens six years in a row. Then it appears on the list, and I really don't give a shit anymore.

## Party Pooper

They gathered at the Red Roof Inn to celebrate Huey Parker's retirement from Mason Tool and Die. A total of 13 fellow employees were there, and when Huey took a head count, he decided someone had to go. Although he wasn't a particularly superstitious guy, he didn't believe in tempting fate, especially on such a symbolic occasion. *People drop dead right after they retire,* he thought. After weighing the pros and cons of those in attendance, he decided that Madeline Hornell, the company owner's secretary, was the best person to oust from his farewell bash. She was not someone he much liked, nor was she popular with anyone else, for that matter. In fact, she gave off an air of superiority that generally irked people. Huey considered how to remove her from the event, and then an idea struck him. He had her number in his cellphone from when he'd called in sick, so he initiated his scheme on the spot. "Hello, Mrs. Hornell? This is Detective Amory calling from police headquarters. Your husband has been in a car accident, and you should go to the hospital emergency room right away to be with him," said Huey, disguising his voice. From where he stood on the other side of the banquet room, he could make out the horrified expression on Madeline's face. *Okay, lady, now make some tracks,* he thought, and as if responding to his command, she began to run for the door. Halfway there, she collapsed, prompting several people to run to her aid. When Huey caught up to the crowd, he heard someone say she wasn't breathing. *The number 13,* he reasoned.

# Mrs. Johnson Is Ready to Greet the Future

His body sagged to one side in the recliner. *He's napping,* she thought, as she approached her husband, gently calling his name. When she was a couple feet away, it occurred to her she might be a widow. *I'll book the penthouse suite in the Ritz at Dorado Beach,* she thought, her pulse quickening.

Michael C. Keith

## VACATIONLAND

Mango Drive led to the swamp where Hank planned to launch his new airboat. On the way, he saw snakes—as well as an occasional alligator—huddled in the dirt road's deep ruts. He'd never seen anything like it. Usually, the sound of an approaching vehicle would send reptiles scampering. The closer he got to his destination, the stranger things looked to him. The typically lush pines and palmettos that dominated the landscape drooped and leaned as if deprived of vital nourishment and the once-dense ground cover was sparse and desiccated—*the whole place looks singed,* he thought. What had been a tropical forest seemed to be morphing into a desert. When he finally reached the water's edge, he was stunned by what he found. The swamp had become a festering caldron spewing noxious odors and dead fish. *My God, what's happened here?* wondered Hank, and then it struck him. *Damn, I took the wrong turn and ended up in Post-Apocalyptic Park.*

## Fourth and Powell

Somebody had been shot at the intersection back in 1953. Nobody in the neighborhood could remember who it was. A forensics student who lived nearby searched through a criminal database as well as local newspapers dating back to the year of the incident and found nothing. He concluded that whoever it was could not have been very important.

*Michael C. Keith*

## Second Thoughts

Glenn Miller's tune, "It's a Blue World," fills the room with its pensive melody. It deepens Meyer's gloom, already deeper than it has ever been. The war is coming to an end, and he's missed out on it so far. There's been nothing he can do to convince the local draft board to recruit him. Yes, he is the last remaining son in his family, his two brothers having lost their lives in the fight. "Why should their sacrifice keep me from serving?" he argues, adding, "I should also be allowed to die for my country." When Meyer's friend informs him the "last son clause" doesn't exempt him from the draft anymore, he decides to forestall his patriotic duty and take a vacation to Canada.

## Compassion Lessons

He collapsed from a brain aneurism while bathing. When his wife heard the loud thud of his body hitting the floor, she ran to the upstairs bathroom. Upon seeing him lying unconscious, she let out a loud, anguished scream. "Oh, my God! You broke the shower curtain rod!"

## When Reason Goes out the Car Window

"Oh, no! This is the kiss of death," moaned Hank.

"What is?" asked his passenger, Gil.

"A Toyota Corolla with a Triple A sticker on it."

"So, what?"

"So, it's a sure indication we're going to crawl along until this slug gets out of our way."

"Well, how do you know that?"

"Who buys one of those dull little shit-boxes and displays a 'Help, I can't change my own tire' sticker on it?" grumbled Hank, pounding on his horn.

"Look, don't get all bent out of shape about it. We'll get there."

"Man, we got ten minutes to reach the liquor store before it closes."

"Calm down. You'll have a stroke. It's not that far away."

"Now, we're down to just eight minutes from closing."

"Okay, run the old fucker off the road."

## Sneaky Pete

"I think I'll work on my painting," answered Estelle, chewing on the remainder of her liverwurst sandwich.

Peter was itching to do something, but, since his wife had plans, he had to come up with something on his own. Nothing came to mind immediately, so he flopped onto the couch and attempted to nap. After a few minutes, he gave up on that idea and took to his reading chair, his latest novel in hand. A half hour later, he lost interest in it and climbed the stairs to his wife's studio.

"You sure you don't want to go somewhere? Maybe antiquing or to the movies?" he asked.

"No, I'm really into this now," she answered, without looking away from her canvas.

About to leave in frustration, Peter came up with an idea. Knowing how much she respected his view of her work, he opined, "Not crazy about what you're doing, honey. Seems a bit derivative."

After a long thoughtful silence, his wife replied. "Where would you like to go?"

*Michael C. Keith*

## It's All in the Numbers

Peterson felt guilty every time he masturbated until he read a report revealing that the average person masturbated three times more than he did.

# The Rapprochement

Religious leaders claimed that prayer was the only hope for preventing a giant meteorite from annihilating the entire human race. When an instant poll was taken to ascertain the percentage of those actually praying, it was concluded that less than half of the world's population was doing so. When the space object actually struck the planet, ministers, rabbis, and imams had no explanation as to why the half that did not pray survived whereas those who did perished. The holy men defended their position by citing the fact that fifty-percent of the Earth's inhabitants remained alive.

Michael C. Keith

## Less Than Expected

When the man regained consciousness after being in a coma for seven years, he had absolutely no memory of his existence on Earth. In fact, he had no idea what it meant to be a human being. When he was told that people were born into this world, lived their lives, and then died, he asked, "What is *died?*" When it was explained to him, a look of incredulity covered his face, and he blurted, "What kind of shit is that?"

# A Statement That Failed to Comfort a Reluctant Flyer

"There's not a thing in the world that doesn't carry with it some risk."

## It's Only a Matter of Time before Your Body Turns Lethal

"Overall, you're doing pretty well," said Dr. Burton, to his longtime patient, Marlon.

"Aside from some aches and pains, I feel okay, doc."

"For seventy-one, I'd say you're holding your own."

Marlon chewed on the doctor's comment for a second and then spoke. "Holding my own, doc…?"

"Well, you know, Marlon, given the stage we all enter if we live long enough."

"What stage is that?"

"Deterioration, Marlon."

# Words Pertaining to the Final Human Indignity

Most people shit themselves moments after they die. Thank you, God, for that. You really could have put a little extra thought into this divine creation thing of yours.

*Michael C. Keith*

# Let Us Now Speak of Extinction

"What is death?" asked the child.

"Ah ... well, it's what happens when you're very old," answered her father.

"And what's it like?"

After a long, awkward pause, the girl's father replied, "Plato said that death is a state of nothingness and utter unconsciousness."

"Oh, I like Play-Doh. So, death is like Play-Doh, Daddy?"

"Yes ... yes, honey, death is exactly like Play-Doh."

## ONE WITH NATURE

I saw a pit viper yawn, and I yawned. It disgusted me that we're related.

*Michael C. Keith*

## SEEKING COUNSEL

I'm an academic advisor. My job is to give students direction as they pursue their studies. *Should I take this course if I plan to major in botany at college? Would this class make sense in a pre-med program?* they ask. In fact, I'm not really sure how sound my recommendations are, but it's my job to provide guidance. So I tell them what to do the way my high school counselor told me what to do.

## Locating Dreams

When Jerry was a kid, he played a game with the map. He'd close his eyes and point to a place, usually in the middle of the country. Then he'd take a look to see where his finger landed. What he'd do next is calculate what was 800 miles to the west of that location. For example, if he touched down in Springfield, Illinois, then he'd be able to go as far as Colorado or Wyoming, which pleased him, because he dreamed of living where there were cowboys. Next, he'd find a town close to where the 800 miles reached (say Sterling, Colorado, or Egbert, Wyoming), and it would be there he'd go to live on a small ranch on its outskirts. After moving to his new home, he'd have his parents buy him a fast horse so he could chase outlaws.

*Michael C. Keith*

# HURT

Because of my pain, the one the surgeons made worse, I inflict pain. I lash out at anyone within the vicinity of my misery. "Honey, would you like a sandwich," she asks, and I bark, "No, for Christ's sake!" For the balance of the day, suffering has more than just me to keep it company.

# The Question That Stumped the Lesser Einstein

He wore an eye patch over his better eye to keep it from becoming as weak as his left one. Which eye was stronger?

Michael C. Keith

## New Movement

They had their time, these Renaissance, Romantic, Transcendental, Victorian, Realist, Naturalist, Modernist, Post-Modernist writers. Forget them. It's good they're gone. It's time to flush the literary bowel ... to clean it for new shit.

# If Wishes Were Buses, Little Girls Would Ride

The seats facing the panoramic windshield on the upper level of the Greyhound SceniCruiser are all the 10-year-old in the Dale Evans cowgirl outfit can think about as she stands in line with her father for their trip to Amarillo. The odds of getting two seats together in such a desirable location are slim to none since several people ahead of her have already boarded the Los Angeles Express. Nonetheless, little Wendy Clark prays there will be empty seats remaining when they get there. The bus driver finally takes their tickets and they climb inside what her imagination has transformed into a stagecoach. For several moments, they wait as passengers settle into their seats in the lower portion of the bus. By the time they reach the steps leading to the elevated section, Wendy's heart is pounding with anticipation. "Please ... please, let there be seats for Daddy and me," she mutters and then spots the denim-clad leg of someone seated on the left side of the upper deck as it comes into view. Her heart sinks, but it takes flight again when she notices the seat on the opposite side of the aisle is vacant. Wendy squeals with delight when she sees the other empty seat. It's the happiest she'll be for the balance of her childhood.

*Michael C. Keith*

## Timeless Injustice

Barry enjoyed posting "Now versus Then" photos of women he knew on Facebook. It amused him to show how much they had aged—how they had lost their youthful qualities. Then one day someone posted a "Now versus Then" photo of him, and he was delighted by how well he'd been treated by time.

## CLIQUES

Unknown writers aspire to join the ranks of well-known writers. Well-known writers are indifferent to the aspirations of unknown writers.

*Michael C. Keith*

## My Final Curtain ...

Will it be a tender occasion?

Will it be a horror realized?

Will it be a tremendous relief?

Will it be a melancholy scene?

Will it be a poignant goodbye?

Will it be a frightful last gasp?

Will it be a shoddy spectacle?

Will it be a storm of regret?

Will it be a blink of an eye?

Will it be a chorus of anger?

Will it be a stirring finale?

Will it be a matter of fact?

Yes ... *yes,* the last one.

# The Joy of Parenthood

He was told not only could he get a new face but he could get a whole new body. He didn't need time to think about it. "Yes," he said, "I'll do it." There was a moment of silence, and then the facilitator asked him if he was completely sure he could take his own child's life to be young again. "It's how we're able to offer you youth. We take from one source and give to another, but the donor has to be a genetic doppelganger and offspring come closest to that. You see why our slogan is 'People with children are fortunate.'"

*Michael C. Keith*

# WHEN ASKED BY POLICE WHY HE DID IT, HE REPLIED:

"Because it feels good to hurt things."

# There Are Times When It Is Difficult to Know What to Believe

"Come down from up there, you damn little fool!" Meghan shouted to her brother from the backyard of what was their recently deceased parent's house. "You can't stay up there forever. Sooner or later you're going to want food or something."

Emil Burton had gone up the slope after his parents were slain. He'd told his sister it would happen, but she wouldn't listen to him, claiming he was having another one of his episodes.

"You're just seeing and hearing things again. Mom and Dad should never have brought you home. I knew you weren't ready. Started acting weird as soon as you got here. They saw it and were thinking about taking you back."

The idea that aliens were out to get them all was plain absurd, she'd thought. Now she wasn't so sure, especially since the pulsating metallic hill behind the house had not been there before her parents died.

*Michael C. Keith*

## Never Stand in the Path of the Wheat Thresher

The jet is a barely discernible silver speck above the western plains. Kevin is standing in the field behind his family's farm covering his eyes from the glare of the sun in an attempt to locate the source of the muffled roar. Finally, he spots it and guesses the plane is going to California, where he plans to live when he grows up ... but he never gets there.

# What If the Iceman Didn't Cometh?

My grandpa delivered ice in Dorchester. Everyone knew and liked Mac—his given name was Irving, but he hated it ... sounded too Jewish to this second-generation Irishman. His wasn't easy work, especially for an old person. At almost 70, he was still lugging 50-pound blocks of ice up the rickety stairs of three-deckers and shoveling coal into furnaces in the evening. My grandma worried that he'd hurt himself, or worse, doing such heavy labor at his age. She tried without success to get him to retire but he wouldn't hear of it, claiming they couldn't make ends meet without his income given it was the middle of the Depression. When I offered to help, my grandpa got all indignant, saying he didn't want my charity. I reminded him that he'd been generous to me my whole life and that I'd like to return it in kind, but he just waved me off and buried his face in his newspaper. As I was heading to the door, he mumbled something I didn't catch. "What, Grandpa?" I asked, and he repeated himself. "My customers depend on me to keep their food from spoiling and their butts from freezing. Can you imagine living without those things? I stop doing what I do, and there's more misery in the world. Isn't there enough already?" he said, pointing to the headline on the front page of his paper, which read: "INVASION FROM MARS CAUSES PANIC."

*Michael C. Keith*

## One Man's Hell

James Baldwin, who spent his life writing and speaking out against racism, died and was reborn into a world where prejudice and injustice were unknown. There he found himself with a lot of time on his hands.

## It Should Happen to Me

*That Warhol guy said everybody gets to be famous for 15 minutes. I haven't yet, and I want to be famous. But how ... how?* The young man wanted celebrity more than anything, and he was even willing to give up his life for it if necessary. Then an idea struck him that he was certain would catapult him to renown while allowing him to remain alive to enjoy his newfound notoriety. His plan involved investing all of his savings in a centrally located, high exposure billboard with his name on it. *Like in that old movie I love with Judy Holiday,* he thought. *Yes ... yes! That will do it. By the time the sign comes down, everybody around here will know the name Kerowichli Vajracheddikaprajanparamita.*

Michael C. Keith

# OBJECTIVELY

At 18, the exclusive club to which I belonged with three other members required we give a secret signal whenever we met. This involved making the sign of the dollar in the air as the protagonist does in *Atlas Shrugged*. We had each read the ponderous tome and thought of ourselves as intellectuals because no one else we knew had slogged through its thousand-plus pages. The fact is we were early geeks and had few associations beyond our tiny circle. When we gathered decades later, only one of us was still an admirer of Rand's work. His defense of her went nowhere fast, and he bid us farewell in a huff. As a parting salvo as he headed away, we raised our hands and with a flourish mimed the author's sacred symbol. In retaliation, our distraught former cohort extended his middle finger. "Was that John Galt?" I offered, and we all chuckled smugly.

## Everlasting Benefit

When you're dead, the good thing is you can stay outside in the winter without your clothes on and not worry about frostbite.

*Michael C. Keith*

## ONE CAN LEARN A GREAT DEAL IN-FLIGHT

Caleb looked down from his window seat 20 thousand feet up and could see why they called it the Big Muddy. He'd wondered why it got that name when his grade school geography teacher used it but failed to mention why. Regrettably, Caleb hadn't asked for an explanation those many years ago. Now he had his answer and felt he'd experienced a major breakthrough in his education.

## Salesman of the Year

Eight inches of snow fell in a one-hour period breaking all previous records in the extreme northwestern corner of Wisconsin. The Kruegers had not anticipated a storm of such magnitude because meteorologists on the local TV channel had predicted a moderate snowfall. Now forecasts were being revised upward, indicating amounts beyond anything ever seen in the region. The state's emergency management agency was in full operation, as was the National Guard and Department of Public Works. People were urged to stay off the roads and take shelter.

"Oh, damn, we're nearly out of milk and bread. Coffee … we need coffee, too. I better get some," said Carolyn Krueger, putting on her coat and grabbing a shovel.

"Whoa, where do you think you're going? It's a blizzard out there. The car's already covered. All you can see is its roof. Look at it. Crazy out there, hon."

Carolyn peered out the window and removed her coat.

"When's this suppose to stop anyway?"

"Not for a while. May get another two feet. I'll start working the snow blower in a while so it's not so bad when it does stop."

When morning arrived, the Kruegers' concerns grew, since forecasters were now talking in terms of the century's worst snowstorm. Adding to the Kruegers' anxiety was the flickering of their house lights.

"We're going to lose electricity. We'll be in the dark. Shit, there they go flickering again," sighed Carolyn.

"Dammit, I should've had the generator repaired. Was going to do it next week but then this happened out of nowhere," grumbled Eric Krueger.

"Lord, heavens, we'll have no heat if we lose power. We'll freeze to death."

"There's some wood outside for the fireplace, if I can get to it. Maybe enough for a couple days."

"It's a total whiteout. Can't see a thing. You better stay put until it lets up," said Carolyn, pacing the living room.

It was then the doorbell rang.

"Who in God's name could that be in this?" muttered Eric, moving to the door and opening it.

"Hello," said a broadly smiling young man clutching a vacuum cleaner. "Does anyone in the house have allergies?"

## Alien Invasion

*What's moving around in my body?* Juan wondered. "Are you friend or foe?" he muttered, clutching at his abdomen. "If the latter, would you please tell me how long it takes for you to dine?"

*Michael C. Keith*

## There Are Some Customers Who Simply Cannot Be Pleased

It took the seriously hungover undertaker most of the morning to reconstruct the accident victim's horribly damaged face. When the next of kin showed up to view the body, she screamed at what she saw.

"What's the problem, Mrs. Griswold?" asked the startled embalmer.

"He would never wear his nose above his ear!"

# Not Exactly the Same Thing

They could not bear the idea of their dead son alone in the mortuary, so they sent his former babysitter over to keep him company for as long as ten dollars would last.

*Michael C. Keith*

## SACRED GROUND

Tahatan Peak was more a mound than anything. You could reach its top in less than 20 minutes and you weren't even winded. It seemed so high because it was the only thing that stood out in our part of the South Dakota plains. We'd go there in the summer because it was cooler than anywhere else … always a nice breeze on top. It was a great place to take your girl to fool around, because you could see if anyone was coming before you got caught. The first time we were going to go all the way, a hawk came screaming down on us out of nowhere, and it wouldn't stop. It scared the heck out of us and we left. That damn bird followed us, too, until we were clear away. Not long after, we broke up. There was something about what happened that changed things between us. Later, I learned that the local Indian tribe used to bury their trash there.

## One of Life's Mysteries

Cassandra had multiple-personality disorder when she slept, so her husband never knew who he was going to be in bed with on any given night.

*Michael C. Keith*

# Absurd

We lived for our trips to the A&W over on Sorenson Street. It usually took us a few weeks to gather the money we needed for burgers and shakes. Most of the time Jake got the dough before me, but he'd wait for me to catch up. Sometimes he got more than he needed before I got what I needed, and he'd give me his extra so we could go sooner. That was ol' Jake, generous to a fault. Best friend I ever had, and I really miss him and didn't mean to kill him. I swear to that. If I could switch places with him, I would in an instant, but you can't change what's done. So, he's in the ground, and I'm in this cell. What he said now seems so benign ... meaningless. Can't explain it but something just snapped in my head when he told me I had no idea what it was to view the world from an existential perspective. Granted, that's a pretty tough thing to be told, *but* ...

# Happy Hour

It happens just before she finishes her martini. A transformation takes place. She sheds her affable nature and becomes hostile and aggressive. A door is opened to her rancor and we begin arguing. Whatever I say, she finds objectionable. It's taken me too long to recognize this pattern, and I've suffered for it. At long last, I'm wise to the warning signs, so I dodge out of the bar and go home. *Let her stay there with her fucking monsters,* I think.

*Michael C. Keith*

## Who's Crying Now?

"How come I never see you cry?" asked his wife.

"Well, I don't want you to think I'm weak and unmanly," he replied.

"Oh, that's not weak and unmanly. Not crying when you should is weak and unmanly."

"I don't know. It just doesn't seem right to me."

"You must cry sometimes. You shouldn't hide your emotions from me."

"It's not something I do, but I'll try to be more open about how I feel. It'll be hard blubbering in front of you, though."

"That's such a strange attitude. I'm the closest person to you. You moan when we have sex, you laugh when I say something funny, you yell when you're mad, so why not cry in front of me when something moves you or makes you sad?"

The years passed without her husband being able to weep in front of her, and then it finally happened … as her body was being removed to the funeral home.

# Noah Manages a Final Journal Entry

*The acid rain keeps falling. It hasn't stopped in three years, and everyone who could has moved to what high ground still exists. The floods have been epic, and, combined with the rising sea levels, we wonder if drowning is in the cards for the few of us who remain. There's been an earth-shaking rumbling coming from the east since yesterday, and we suspect it may be the end-times tsunami we all knew would eventually roll across the last of the land masses.*

*Michael C. Keith*

## WHAT THE RABBI TOLD HIM MOMENTARILY STILLED HIS FEARS

"The best thing about being dead is you don't know you're dead. And if you do know you're dead, well, that isn't bad either."

# Tea Time

Sheba Levesque consumed half a dozen cups of tea a day, and had for most of her adult life. It sustained her, and without it she wasn't herself. On the one occasion she fell short of her required quota, her appearance became altered in a way that startled those around her. Her face turned dark purple, and her nose and lips became bulbous and grotesque. Fortunately, the condition only lasted a few minutes, but long enough to impress her with the restorative power of a fine pekoe.

*Michael C. Keith*

## AGE NON SEQUITUR

He would have been 80 today if he hadn't died at 76.

## The Enchanting Hereafter

At 87, Carson knew he was on death's shortlist. "About run out of my supply of tomorrows," he'd note when people asked how he was. When the news broke that a pill designed to reverse aging was about to appear on the market, he pooh-poohed the idea of taking it. "So what am I going to gain by sticking around? More of the same old same old, is what I think. Could be something magical on the other side." When he died a short time later, his friends questioned his decision to reject the youth-restorer. However, unbeknownst to them, Carson was able to listen in on their conversation from his casket in the frozen ground. "Not the magic I had in mind," he thought.

*Michael C. Keith*

## Pointers from Papa

Hemingway urged writers to start with one true sentence, and wannabe author Seymour Hayden took the legendary scribe at his word. He planned to pen an episodic novel based on his great-uncle's exploits aboard a tramp steamer in the South Pacific. After countless false starts and misfires, he finally found the sentence that for him most accurately embodied Hemingway's famous maxim: "I can't write worth a shit."

## Passing It Along

The ill-informed parents took their anger and frustration out on their children, who would also grow into ill-informed, angry and frustrated parents who would take their anger and frustration out on their children ...

*Michael C. Keith*

## PROFOUND DISCOURSE AT A DUNKIN

"When contemplating the nature of human existence, it's very easy to reach the conclusion that the whole thing is a cruel absurdity," said Gill.

"Oh, jeez, fellas, Gill is getting all existential on us. What do you expect us to do with that information?" replied Doug, winking at fellow members of the Somerville Old Farts Breakfast Club.

"Well," answered Gill, "You could add meaning to my life by buying me another Vanilla Frosted with Sprinkles."

## Something Left to Brag About

Teeth ... teeth are something I have better than most my age. Maybe not the best hair or best skin or best body, but teeth ... yes, teeth are something I have better than most folks my age.

*Michael C. Keith*

## On a Late Sunday Afternoon

There are mounds of decaying leaves scattered across the lawn of the deserted house—the house where two young girls were defiled and murdered. My friend wants to go inside and chase their ghosts into the open. He says that would be great fun. I tell him I think the ghosts are under the piles of dead leaves, and he kicks through them with childlike abandon until his foot strikes something hard, and he falls to the ground in pain. "Goddamn ghosts!" he growls, clutching his L. L. Bean hiking boot.

## Paradise Lost

The persistent roll of the Big Horn zephyrs across the northern Wyoming lowlands helped form its unique, mushroom-shaped sandstone outcroppings. It was this geological anomaly that attracted extraterrestrials from a planet whose principal diet was fungi of the *Agaricus* genus. Given the growing scarcity of their primary food supply, due to a virulent microbe of unknown origin, the aliens were excited by this discovery. However, not long after landing, they were forced to return to their home planet for emergency dental work.

*Michael C. Keith*

## Strategy for Living

Merle kept a Xanax in his watch pocket in case he got the screaming fantods, as he called them. A couple times he'd reached for the little football-shaped pill but managed to hold off taking it. That act alone had calmed his frantic heart enough to keep him from jumping out of the moving car.

## Down the Toilet

Clyde was alarmed to find the commode stained with fecal matter. When he emerged from the bathroom belonging to the woman he'd only been out with one other time, she greeted him with a warm smile announcing she was ready to go to dinner. Dismayed by what he'd just seen, he said he couldn't date her anymore. Taken aback, she asked why. He thought about what to say for a moment and decided to be forthright. "I can tell from your poop you're not my type. I can't imagine spending time with a person who condones the slaughter of cattle." She looked at him perplexed and asked what he meant. "Your stool has the telltale sign of beef in it, and I don't eat beef, so we're clearly incompatible." Affronted by Clyde's assertion, the woman countered, "And I can't imagine having a relationship with a person who doesn't know the difference between beef and pork."

*Michael C. Keith*

## Afterlife

He had been pronounced dead seven hours earlier, but he still felt something—a slight twitch in his right-hand pinky finger.

## Hospital Roommates with Contrasting Perspectives

"Of all the illnesses you can get, the one I'd like is tonsillitis, because they give you ice cream," said Brian.

"Well, of all the diseases you can get, the one I'd like is late-stage cancer, because they give you morphine," replied Joel.

*Michael C. Keith*

# Scything You Up

At 70, you have to work hard to stave off death. You take your vitamins, avoid fatty foods, and move your limbs as much as possible. Do all the things your doctor tells you. But whatever it is that's causing your body to sag and hobble has already figured out what it needs to finish you off.

## Six-Foot Variance

Most of us try to be *something* during our time above ground—what Kurt Vonnegut called the "Universal Will to Become." But when we run out of time, we spend eternity being *nothing* underground.

*Michael C. Keith*

## There Are Times When You Have to Try a Little Harder

He did everything she wanted and she still wasn't happy. This frustrated him greatly, because more than anything he wanted her to be happy. "Just tell me your fondest wish, and I'll try to make it come true," he asked. "Well, if you really mean it, I think I would be happy with you dead, a beautiful house, and a really hot boyfriend." It hurt him to hear his wife say that, but he was committed to her happiness no matter what. "Okay," he replied, "I can get you two of those things, but the beautiful house is going to be hard."

# Misconception

I'm too naïve to recognize that my friends, a young man and a young woman, are interested in a threesome. Later when I realize this, I think of it as a missed opportunity to have played Scrabble with them.

*Michael C. Keith*

## SENSIBLE EATING AND LONG LIFE

Marty's doctor strongly urged him to avoid consuming so much red meat, but it was the one food he loved above all others. On a typical day, he devoured a couple pounds of beef. And all too often his consumption of meat exceeded that. Compounding the danger his intake of red meat posed, he preferred his steaks as undercooked as he could get them. What restaurants considered rare didn't come close to what he wanted. In fact, when he ate at home, he didn't bother cooking his meat at all. His preparation of a meal simply involved removing the wrapper from a roast and serving it up raw. After years of this type of diet, he came down with several chronic conditions his doctor attributed to his reckless eating habit. "You'll never make it to your next birthday if you keep it up," he warned. To which his patient replied, "Who wants to be a hundred anyway?"

## Vlad's Repast

The young man sitting across from me at Sir Reginald's dinner party was not aware that I was stealing some of his life. I can do that, you know.

*Michael C. Keith*

## WE ALL HAVE SOMETHING IN COMMON

This Asian guy in civvies is sitting across from me in the galley of the troop ship that's headed to Korea in 1962. "How come you're here, buddy? You ain't a soldier, right?" I ask. He looks up from his tray and says he's being deported. "Deported … why?" After taking a sip from his coffee mug, he says it's because he's a Marxist. I tell him that's crazy, because I'm a marksman, too.

# The Socially Conscious Sixties

Sam's 1954 Ford Victoria blew a rod near the Glades Shopping Plaza on 183rd Street in Carol City. It was 12 years old when that happened and had 81 thousand miles on its odometer, a lot for cars back then. He couldn't leave it on the street where it broke down, so he got a push into the parking lot near Sears. He then removed his registration from the glove compartment and took off the license plates. *There,* he thought, *it's not my problem anymore.*

*Michael C. Keith*

## METHOD OF RECONCILIATION

Matthew found if he touched his wife's forehead at her temple, while she slept, it would draw her dreams to the surface. She would rant on and on about how marrying him was a mistake. How it had ruined her life. How he spoiled everything. Then it occurred to him never to touch her again ... at least nowhere near her brain.

## Nietzsche said, "Without music, life would be a mistake."

Playing the saxophone kept Buddy from succumbing to the gloom that often accompanies the work of a mortician. Many of his industry friends suffered from bouts of depression, and he'd flirted with it as well until he renewed his interest in music. He'd put aside his favorite pastime for several years to focus on building his business. Now he spent as much time as possible performing with a local band. He regarded it as his salvation, and his appreciation for the benefits of song grew enormously when he brought his favorite recordings into the embalming room. However, Buddy found it was necessary to shut off the music when draining his client's fluids. Attempting that task while dancing with a body was impossible.

*Michael C. Keith*

## HOUDINI HAS A JARRING WAKE-UP CALL

There was no trap he couldn't escape, or so he thought. Then one morning he woke up with the distressing thought he would die one day and could do nothing to avoid it. The awareness was a devastating punch to the solar plexus of the renowned illusionist.

# Late Afternoon of the Writer's Day

Anne waits for a better idea. She's had lesser ones all day. A series of false starts. A line or two, even a short paragraph, but nothing really going anywhere ... so DELETE! Blank page, again. She continues to wait. Sunset comes and she paces. *Not another lost day,* she frets, deadline looming. *Shit! Shit! Shit!* She pours herself a drink and then a second. More idle hours pass. When she sees it's midnight, she brightens. *Okay, it could happen today. No, it* will *happen today,* she tells herself, emptying the Dewar's bottle.

## Friends with Solutions

"What do you do when people won't even pick up litter and trash on the street in front of their own house?" asked Howard.

"Good question," replied his pal.

"Americans are such slobs, so disrespectful of the environment. They chuck garbage out of their car windows and dispose of junk on public and private property without the slightest regard for what it looks like. Hell, they even heave crap out in their own yards. What the hell do you do about that?"

"You set fire to their houses."

## INTERSPECTION

I recently asked myself: *What do you do, Sol? I mean, what are you about?* And my answer to myself was: *I work on things. Little things, you might say. Pieces about life really. All aspects of existence but about death in particular.* So that's what I do. That's how I spend most of my conscious hours, some of my dreamtime, too. Put another way, what I do is work on things that have to do with my thoughts, which are mostly about death and dying. *This is good,* I think … examining what it is I do. Now I understand why I'm so depressed most of the time.

*Michael C. Keith*

## A Tasteless Offense

Had he done everything he could to hide the evidence? As far as he could tell, he had. But he knew from watching thousands of television detectives that there was always something left behind to nail the culprit. *Go over the scene again,* he told himself. *Look for anything that may provide clues to what you did.* He carefully scanned the kitchen where his unsavory act occurred. He ran the palm of his hand over the countertop making sure there was nothing left behind, nothing he'd overlooked. Then he did the same to the floor near the refrigerator and along the base of the counter. *Clean ... it's totally clean,* he told himself, lifting himself from his kneeling position. *Maybe I should remove any fingerprints,* he thought, but then figured it was unnecessary since it was his kitchen and the presence of his fingerprints would not be incriminating. He stood in silence for several minutes and finally came to the realization that he couldn't live with the guilt he felt; that he had to come clean to his wife about eating the last portion of the low-fat haggis—her favorite.

## Just Look at Us

We die of cancer, heart attacks, and wars. Our life spans are infinitesimal, and the most reliable evidence available shows that we ultimately end up as ash—*quintessence of dust*. Yes, just look at us, as we ignore the reality of human existence and continue to strive despite the lousy payoff.

*Michael C. Keith*

## 3 AM

Just before I wake up I'm dreaming someone is bouncing a rubber ball against my house. When I do wake up, I go to the bathroom. It's the third time, I remind myself. On my way back to bed, I look out the window, half-expecting to see someone. At the corner stoplight, a car waits. Before the light turns green, it pulls away. A ball trails after it, bounding skyward every few feet.

## Accessory

Gerald didn't want to die in the electric chair for a crime he had hardly committed. If his friend hadn't loaned him a gun with a hair trigger, he wouldn't be in this terrible situation. He felt it was a gross injustice to execute him because the goddamn .38 had a mind of its own.

## Nature Boy

Harvey's favorite singer was Nat King Cole, but he possessed a general disdain for black people. When his friend asked him how he could love and hate the same person, he was at a loss to provide an answer. Over the next several days, Harvey examined his views on race but could come to no reasonable explanation as to why he felt the way he did. However, believing he needed to do something proactive to address the dichotomy in his attitude toward people of a different color, he decided to throw away his collection of the famous crooner's records.

# Thoughts That Keep Them Awake

We're watching each other grow old. Which is another way of saying we're watching each other die. We would choose to spend our time another way. But it's not like we have an option.

*Michael C. Keith*

## Things Always Make More Sense in the Morning

Marvin used to get up in the middle of the night to have a smoke ... but no more. After decades, he finally quit. Now he gets up in the middle of the night because something outside his house rouses him. It isn't a noise that disturbs him, but rather a light so intense that it invades his dreams. When he makes his way to his bedroom window to check it out, he's not sure whether he's seeing a spacecraft, a group of nuns, or his long-deceased mother. Unable to figure it out, he returns to bed and sleep. When he wakes up in the morning, it's clear to him what got him up hours before. He goes to the front door and waves his mother inside.

# Someone Has an Emergency and Triggers a Paranoid Reaction

There was a murderous presence down the road, and Russ wondered how long it had been there. It wasn't until a new-model powder-blue Camry nearly hit him as he backed out of his driveway (and then tore around him at breakneck speed) that he knew something malevolent had moved into his neighborhood. He figured the only way to keep from being victimized by it was to make the first move—a preemptive strike. And he planned to do just that.

*Michael C. Keith*

## SHE ASKED THIS QUESTION ON OUR FIRST DATE

"You ever notice when the sunlight hits an object just right you're transported back to a time when the snow smells like roses?"

# It's Good When God Favors You

The wall of dust came roaring in from the west Texas plains. Bernice sealed the windows in her trailer with towels and old blankets to keep the sand from seeping in and covering everything. Like the last time, she prayed that the force of the wind would not destroy her home. It had flipped her neighbor's Winnebago, and she had felt blessed that the Lord had chosen to honor *her* request.

*Michael C. Keith*

## OLD FRIENDS ON THE ROAD, AGAIN

We're going to spend a week in Wyoming. Drive the two-lane blacktops through the wide-open spaces. How many more times will we do this, I wonder, given we're both pushing 70? We love America's west, even though I'm a native Bostonian and my friend lives in Sri Lanka. We'll meet up in Denver and take a rental to the northern border of Wyoming. Maybe venture into Montana to Little Big Horn. We've been there before but share an urge to return. Maybe it's our last stand, too.

## The Harsh Realist

"Everything in the world goes away, son."

"Even the mountains and the oceans?"

"Yes, even them."

"What about the trees and animals?"

"Them, too."

"And the airplanes and pyramids?"

"Certainly ... everything."

"Even McDonalds and the Statue of Liberty?"

"Afraid so, son."

"All the Eskimos and You Tube, too?"

"Yup, gone ... vanished."

"How about Disney World?"

"Afraid so ... like everything else."

"And the drivers who stick their finger out at us when we're in our car?"

"No, son, not them. There will *always* be assholes."

*Michael C. Keith*

## Parental Care

It took 20 minutes to dig the splinter out of the little boy's finger. The instrument his father used to extract it was a dirty blade in his old Swiss knife. A week later the child's finger had become infected, so his father used an unsanitary needle to pierce the blister and remove the pus it contained. Three days after that, the nine-year-old ran a high fever and his father immersed him in a tub of icy water to bring down the temperature. This resulted in his contracting pneumonia. For several days, the boy hovered on the edge of death and when he finally appeared to be recovering, he beckoned his father to his side and uttered, "Stay the fuck away from me."

# The Joy *That* Publishing Brings

I read through my latest book just published by a tiny press. I'm upset to find it still needs tweaking. Its publisher has done little or no copyediting, and it's too late to rid the volume of its unnecessary relative pronouns. A second printing could address the issue, but there will be no second printing by a press that's done so little with the first printing.

*Michael C. Keith*

## Belated Mourning

While Gary was scanning the obit page in his newspaper, he wondered how many of the people he'd lost contact with throughout his life had already died. He was 72 so figured a good many of those he'd known when he was younger were gone, because most had been older than him. It was then that he gave voice to the overwhelming sense of despair and regret that seized him. *The food at some of those wakes was probably excellent!*

# Stretching the Limits of Acceptance

When the plane descended over Minneapolis/St. Paul on its way to Istanbul, the pilot announced he'd drifted off course and asked if passengers would settle for a few days in the Land of 10,000 Lakes. After a short pause, a loud cheer went up in the cabin.

*Michael C. Keith*

# An Imagined Conversation between Janis, Jim and Jimi in 2020

Janis: So cool to see you boys again, but I have to admit you don't look too groovy.

Jim: Fifty years takes a toll, Mama. What'd you expect? Aging does a number on you.

Jimi: I feel like crap. Joints ache, and I can't eat a thing without getting heartburn.

Janis: Tell me about it. I'm on a dozen meds just to keep me from crashing.

Jim: Got this heart condition, you know. An irregular beat, says the doc.

Janis: What happened to your beautiful hair, Mr. Mojo?

Jimi: Yeah, and that potbelly don't look very cool either, Jim.

Janis: Both you guys used to be gods. I wanted to have you … or maybe I did?

Jimi: Another thing about being old: memory is fried. Can't remember all the good times.

Jim: Must be a real bummer to get old.

Janis: Lucky we didn't, man.

Jimi: Right on, Pearl!

Jim: Far out!

Michael C. Keith

## EVERYTHING OLD IS NEW, AGAIN

A middle-aged man in Rochester, New York, had no day-to-day recall of what he'd read. While it frustrated him that his unusual condition prevented him from finishing a novel and starting another, his wife was pleased that his leisure-time activity placed no demand on their expendable income.

# In Response to Tragic News of a Global Nature

CNN's website featured its major headline of the moment in red across the top of the screen. It read: MUDSLIDE KILLS 98 PEOPLE IN COLOMBO. The "x" in the banner allowed one to delete it.

*Michael C. Keith*

# You Must Plan Ahead When You're Not Quite Like Indigenous Life Forms

Two and a half hours remained in the flight, and there was no way I was getting past the two obese Earthlings next to me. I swore to myself I would only take an aisle seat on future flights. It was just plain foolish of me to sit by a window when my inner particle accelerator could collide if I were denied a waste extrusion.

## Sacrificing for Art

After I fight with my wife, I can write. But I don't like fighting with my wife. I do like to write, though, and sometimes it's hard to write if I don't fight with my wife, so I fight with my wife so I can write.

*Michael C. Keith*

# IMPOSITION

We're walking up to the abandoned cabin where we slip away to have sex, when we see a candle flickering inside. We move a few steps closer, wondering who could be using our secret rendezvous, when we see a naked woman standing in the window and a naked man joining her. The two lock in a passionate embrace and then disappear. It's not that we recognize them as our spouses that angers us, but rather the fact that now we'll have to find someplace else to carry out our infidelities.

# Highway to Heaven

For the hell of it, Kyle asked his GPS for directions to Heaven. The response he received gave him pause:

> *Take steps to reduce your offensive behavior and make amends for all the harm you've done.*

Michael C. Keith

## BEDEVILED

Think of yourself as an egg. You're placed into a pot of boiling water and left there until you harden. Then you're stripped of your shell and halved lengthwise. Your yoke is removed and mashed into a fine crumble with a fork. Next your smashed innards are mixed with mayo, vinegar, mustard, salt, and pepper and stuffed back into the albumen that once helped guard your sovereignty.

# The Benefits of a Creative Imagination

After rising hours before dawn and rushing to return his rental and check-in at the airport, Harry found his flight had been delayed. This meant he'd have to hang around for nearly five hours before takeoff. He took a seat near his airline's ticket counter, which was yet to open, and settled in to draft a story. It would be based on the experience at hand and feature a character much like himself. After several unsuccessful starts, he grew sleepy and drifted off. When he woke up, he was pleased to see he'd napped to his departure time. *Writing can be the best way to pass the hours,* he thought.

## Animal on the Run

Nellie made a break for it. She'd had enough of having her teats pulled and squeezed. The old farmer just didn't know how painful it was, or didn't care, and she simply couldn't take it anymore. So she ran as soon as she saw an opportunity. And she planned to keep on running. *So far, so good*, she thought, as she slipped on and off the subway relatively unnoticed.

# Eternal Question

I'm going back to not being here ... to not *being*. I was that before I *was*. Should that worry me now that I *am?*

## Maybe God?

The *New York Times* featured a photograph of the rings of Saturn taken by the spacecraft *Cassini*. The preciseness of their arcs and their delicate tonality struck Kyle. *Tell me those weren't deliberately designed,* he thought, feeling a little less anxious about his terminal illness.

# Upon Discovering that Author Larry Brown Died in 2004, I Think ...

*Thirteen years is a long time to be dead. Do readers resurrect you, or is it just a myth that writers live on through their words?*

*Michael C. Keith*

## PRIDE FOR THINGS NOT YOURS

For the third year in a row, Down Under Sweetie won Best in Show in her K9 category. Her owner, Sarah Cogswell, gloried in her Airedale Terrier's renown and made it known to all that her canine's distinction belonged to her alone.

# What Was Outside Comes In

Tom awoke from a sound sleep sensing he was in imminent danger. That there was something on the street in front of his house that had come for him. For a moment, he was too frightened to leave his bed. A sudden flash of intense light and a deep rumbling caused his body to stiffen and his fingers to clutch the sheets. For several moments, he lay frozen, fearing he would be detected by whatever it was. Finally he slipped from bed and moved to the window, where he peeked out from behind the curtain. A hooded figure looked up at him from the sidewalk, and he leapt back, a putrid breath against his neck.

*Michael C. Keith*

## Senior Conundrum

Judith couldn't remember taking her pills shortly after she'd taken them. This was of great concern to her; she feared that she might be missing her pills entirely or double-dosing on them. Finally, at her friend's suggestion, she bought a pill dispenser as a means for gaining control over the situation. When she returned home from the drugstore, she carefully filled all seven compartments of the pill dispenser. It was Tuesday, and she looked at the slot she'd just filled for that day and wondered if she'd already taken her Tuesday pills.

## Afterwords

Let me hold my book in my grave and hope someone will dig me up and read it.

# About the Author

MICHAEL C. KEITH is the author or coauthor of more than two dozen groundbreaking books on electronic media, among them *Talking Radio, Voices in the Purple Haze, Sounds of Change, The Broadcast Century, Radio Cultures, Signals in the Air,* the classic textbook *The Radio Station* (later *Keith's Radio Station*), and *Waves of Rancor*—a book cited by President Clinton for its study of the radical right's use of audio media. The recipient of numerous awards in the academic field, including the Broadcast Education Association's Lifetime Achievement Award, the International Radio Television Society's Stanton Fellow Award, and the University of Rhode Island's Achievement Award in the Humanities, he is also the author of dozens of articles and short stories and has served in a variety of editorial positions. Prior to joining Boston College (where he was named Emeritus upon retiring), Michael served as Chair of Education at the Museum of Broadcast Communications and on the faculties of The George Washington University, Marquette University, and Dean College. He is co-founder of the Broadcast Education Association's Radio Division, and its first chair. Beyond that, he is the author of an acclaimed memoir, *The Next Better Place* (Algonquin Books); a young adult novel, *Life is Falling Sideways;* and 14 story collections: *Of Night and Light, Everything is Epic, Sad Boy, And Through the Trembling Air, Hoag's Object, The Collector of Tears, If Things Were Made To Last Forever, Caricatures, The Near Enough, Bits, Specks, Crumbs, Flecks, Slow Transit, Perspective Drifts Like a Log on a River,* and *Stories in the Key of Me.* He has been nominated a half dozen times for a Pushcart Prize and was a finalist for the National Indie Excellence Award for short fiction anthology and a finalist for the 2013 International Book Award in the "Fiction Visionary" category. www.michaelckeith.com

www.ingramcontent.com/pod-product-compliance
Lightning Source LLC
Chambersburg PA
CBHW020328170426
43200CB00006B/304